PENGUIN BOOKS

"MAC"

Elliott Carlisle is professor of management at the University of Massachusetts. Born in Canada, he was educated at McGill University and the University of Michigan, where he received his Ph.D. He is an active management consultant as well as a teacher and a writer. Like the narrator of *"Mac,"* he is an inveterate plane traveler and a connoisseur of fine Scotch.

"MAC"

Managers Talk About Managing People

Elliott Carlisle

PENGUIN BOOKS

PENGUIN BOOKS
Viking Penguin Inc., 40 West 23rd Street,
New York, New York 10010, U.S.A.
Penguin Books Ltd, Harmondsworth,
Middlesex, England
Penguin Books Australia Ltd, Ringwood,
Victoria, Australia
Penguin Books Canada Limited, 2801 John Street,
Markham, Ontario, Canada L3R 1B4
Penguin Books (N.Z.) Ltd, 182–190 Wairau Road,
Auckland 10, New Zealand

First published in the United States of America by
McGraw-Hill Book Company 1983
Published by Viking Penguin Inc. 1985
by arrangement with McGraw-Hill Book Company

LIBRARY OF CONGRESS CATALOGING IN PUBLICATION DATA
Carlisle, Elliott.
"Mac," managers talk about managing people.
Reprint. Originally published: New York: McGraw-Hill,
c1983.
Includes bibliographical references.
1. Industrial management. I. Title.
[HD31.C344 1984] 658 84-335
ISBN 0 14 00.7315 9

Printed in the United States of America by
R. R. Donnelley & Sons Company, Harrisonburg, Virginia
Set in Aster

Chapter 1 first appeared as "The Golfer" in *California Management Review*, vol. 22, no. 1, Fall 1979, pp. 42–52, and is reprinted by permission of the Regents of the University of California.

TO FLOYD LANTZ

PREFACE

THERE IS a distressing tendency to play down the role of judgment in managerial decision making and implementation and to favor what Jerome Bruner calls the "left side of the brain" with its emphasis on hard data and deductive reasoning.[1]

Perhaps the emergence of contingency management, with its inherent flexibility of approach, is an acknowledgment that iron-clad rules have failed to solve the problems encountered by managers in performing one essential part of their task: dealing with people. But more than psychology is involved, because there is simply no substitute for managerial judgment.

Management is a topic of considerable interest to some of us and of vital interest to all of us. Discussing some of the problems encountered by today's managers, *"Mac"* proposes various approaches, but it deliberately leaves final solutions up to the reader. The aim of these essays is simply to present the differing perspectives of several admittedly biased practitioners in the field, which has aptly been described as a "social necessity."[2]

Elliott Carlisle
Céret, France

CONTENTS

FOREWORD

BACK IN THE summer of 1976 an article appeared in *Organizational Dynamics* which didn't fit the usual format of that professional journal. Elliott Carlisle, a senior professor at the University of Massachusetts, was its author; its title, simply, "MacGregor." It was an instant hit; people began to talk about it and copies proliferated. Training directors bought reprints to distribute to their managers and stole more by means of the local copy machine. What was surprising about that article, which promises to become a classic in management writing, was its special *parable* format. Now, parables aren't new, for they are plentiful in the New Testament, and have shown up in other works over the ensuing millennia. Sometimes the parables are about animals who act like people, as in George Orwell's *Animal Farm*, or imaginary dwarfs and giants like Jonathan Swift's *Gulliver's Travels*. When the people warred against their conquerers they wrote parables or fables which made wolves of the conquerers and noble animals of the oppressed. Usually the oppressed won.

A parable, you see, sets forth moral or spiritual precepts by telling about something that might occur naturally. What Carlisle did superbly and for the first time was to write a parable about something that might happen naturally in an executive setting, describing executive behavior as it should be through a tale.

Carlisle's parable produced a rash of requests from editors, including some from the most prestigious and widely read management and business journals, for more parabolic teaching. It also stimulated a rash of other writings using the form with varying degrees of skill. The most popular of these is *The One Minute Manager*, which at this writing basks on *The New York Times* best-seller list for its fifteenth week. Its author, Kenneth Blanchard, freely admits that his work is inspired by Carlisle's. I suppose this could lead to a lot of furor about who invented what first, but that's trivial. Both are fine books, but the record should state that in 1976 Carlisle established parabolic teaching as one of the most exciting new ideas in management education and training. You can likewise bet that for the rest of the decade every writer, consultant, and assistant professor with access to a typewriter or word processor will be rushing to print with his or her own parables. In short, you have the makings of a new school of training, a new genre of management writing, and in the pages that follow you can read with the feeling that you are treading newly plowed ground.

"*Mac*" is different from dry-as-dust Harvard case studies replete with accounting charts and pedantic analyses by competent but boring writers. For the parable is first a ripping good tale. That's one limitation on their proliferation, though, for only skilled writers can pull them off. God knows they are few in academia. A good parable is also interesting because of the characters who inhabit it. Parables cry out to be told over and over, like the *Tales of a Wayside Inn*. Like Aesop's fables they really should be read aloud, and passed along by word of mouth. Thus this book, with characters named MacCormick, or MacGuffy, or MacDuff, or somebody else whose name, by marvelous coincidence, starts with Mac. The people who hold the conversations which make up the book are obviously professional managers, and damned well informed at that. Gulliver had never read Henry Mintzberg, nor could he talk with sophistication about Peter Drucker or contingency theories of management like the Macs in this book can. The parables contained herein could only have been written by a mature and experienced management professor about mature and experienced managers at the higher levels of the organization.

Arthur Elliott Carlisle ("Call me Elliott") has always been a superior writer. Perhaps his youthful experience as a reporter for the Windsor (Ontario) *Daily Star*, plus business experience at Ford of Canada and The Stroh Brewery Company, plus a classical education, sharpened that skill. When I first met him at the University of Michigan twenty years ago I was awed by his facility with words. But his published articles and books have been regrettably few. Then he arrived at the age which people consider mature, in fact darn near a guru. To my great pleasure—and, I am confident, yours as well—I discovered that he has launched management education by parable.

Make no mistake about parables. The fact that they are simple in appearance doesn't mean they deal with simple topics, but rather that they make the complex, the uncertain, and the obscure seem simple. One of these parables has appeared in film.* Like me, perhaps you learn more about managing by watching an exem-

---

* *A Case of Working Harder, Not Smarter*, CRM/McGraw-Hill.

plary performer than you do by reading regression analysis of data-based interventions and questionnaires, and if so you will look forward to more Macs appearing in the future. Perhaps MacDonald, MacLean, and MacKay will join MacDuff and the rest to tell us in plain talk what successful executives do and how business can succeed, to show us the real problems real executives confront.

George S. Odiorne
University of Massachusetts
Amherst, Massachusetts

"MAC"

MacCallum

I WAS SITTING in a window seat on the Detroit–New York flight when I saw MacCallum. He was slightly above average height, with an athletic air about him, and the balding top of his head was freckled and tanned. But what immediately set him apart from the rest of the passengers, predominantly businesspeople, was his air of relaxation and composure: in a word, he seemed to have everything under control. Briefly surveying the empty seats from the cabin door, he made his way to the one next to mine.

The plane took off almost immediately, and I embarked on some last-minute work that I had to have completed before the meeting the next morning, but I couldn't help noticing out of the corner of my eye that my neighbor seemed to be making a series of calculations based on a small pack of golf scorecards retrieved from an inside pocket. When I glanced up at him, he confided, "I have to get my handicap figured out before the tournament tomorrow."

"Are you a professional golfer?" I asked.

"No," he replied, "but I play a lot of golf. You can never be any good at the game if you only play on weekends. Actually I'm in the oil business; I run a refinery. MacCallum is the name, how about you?"

I introduced myself, and we chatted about business in general and mine in particular—operating a screw machine products plant outside of Toledo. He was such a good listener that before long I found myself unloading all my work-related problems, which centered on my inability to find enough time to respond adequately and calmly to the seemingly endless demands of my job.

Finally, I asked him whether he didn't ever have the same problem.

"I used to be rushed off my feet all the time," he replied with half a smile, "but not any more. In fact, it was about five years ago that my golf game began to deteriorate, and I decided I had to do something about it, so that's exactly what I did. If you can put aside the work you're doing, which, by the way, probably should have been assigned to one of your subordinates, and if you're really interested, I'll tell you how I went about it."

I certainly was interested. His comment about my work was true, but I never seemed to have the time to train my subordinates so they could take on more of my work load. Not only did I seem to be scrambling harder and harder, but my golf scores were slipping too! So I sat back and decided that I might learn something from MacCallum. I could get up an hour earlier tomorrow and finish the work I'd scheduled for the plane ride.

"Before I took my present job," he began, "I ran a much smaller operation for the same company— roughly half the size of the one I have now—and I was nearly going out of my mind. Every two or three minutes either the telephone would ring and interrupt my train of thought or someone would appear outside and tell my secretary that it was absolutely essential that he or she talk with me about a matter of such crucial importance that dire consequences would result from the slightest delay. In fact, it usually turned out that the cause of the interruption was a problem that should have been dealt with at a lower organizational level. But in addition to the precious time I lost to the unnecessary intrusion itself, I needed even more time to recover my train of thought afterwards, and all too often I never got back to where I was with my thinking before someone else broke in on me, and the pattern started again."

"That's exactly my problem," I replied, "and it seems to be a common one. I remember an article by Henry Mintzberg in the *Harvard Business Review* where he cites his studies showing that managers work in a frantic rather than an orderly manner,[1] and he sums up my life as a manager in a word: frantic.

"How did you go about developing your new approach to management?"

"Oh, it's not particularly new, and it's really not mine; in fact, it simply involves going back to basics. The essential job of management is making and implementing decisions in such a way that the organization can reach its objectives. No problem there. Every manager knows that, in theory, at least, organizational objectives have to be established, broken down into meaningful goals, and then communicated to and accepted by organizational members. As you know, they often fail to achieve this acceptance, but more about that later. Typically, we managers forget that, as Stanley Young puts it, a primary responsibility, if not *the* primary responsibility of management, is to design and maintain the management system.[2] And, failing that, most managers at all organizational levels are frantically busy doing tasks that should fall to their subordinates simply because they have not had the time, or perhaps more accurately, have not taken the time to think coldly about their jobs and the nature of their organizational responsibilities. To make matters even worse, they fail to recognize that, often unconsciously, they're spending their time on activities that they have always enjoyed rather than directing their efforts toward those responsibilities for which they're being paid a premium over their subordinates. Like the early Jersey Standard executives described by Alfred Chandler, they focus their day-to-day interests on the immediate and not the long-range problems. They prefer action to analysis."[3]

"How do you mean?" I asked. "Everyone realizes that managers get paid according to responsibility—the greater their responsibility, the higher their pay."

"That's right, but it doesn't go far enough," replied MacCallum. "Upper level managers usually have more responsibility, but it's more than that. They're paid a premium because successfully achieving organizational goals at these levels includes additional responsibilities, among them the design, development, and maintenance of a system which enables their units to operate with maximum effectiveness, as well as that uniquely managerial and often postponed activity called *planning*. Because managers usually neglect this organizational design aspect of their jobs, work structures and relationships evolve on their own, despite the efforts of formally appointed organizational designers. But they pay heavily for this neglect by having to take on an additional work load. Another often slighted side of the middle- and upper-level manager's job is the implementation of control mechanisms used by the entire unit— not just the accountants and systems people—to monitor organizational performance and to take steps at the most appropriate level to adjust operations to standards. In a nutshell," he added with a wry smile, "most managers, and from the worried expression on your face you're no exception, neglect these duties to their own misfortune and to the detriment of their golf games. Maybe I can show you better what I mean by slightly modifying a diagram you've no doubt been exposed to before."

He reached into his pocket for an envelope and made a sketch on the back like the following chart.[4]

Work and Free Time Available to Managers

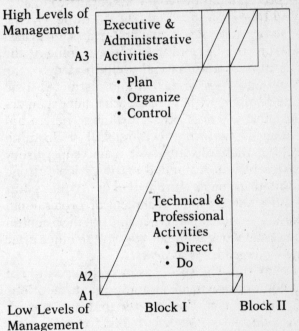

Block I represents time a manager spends on work-related activities.
Block II represents available free time.

"The diagram shows all the time available to a manager, both on and off the job, the broad classes of his or her responsibilities, and the activities performed to carry out these responsibilities. At entry-level 'Managerial' position A1, virtually all work time is spent on technical or professional duties, which is perfectly appropriate, since a new person is added to the staff because of his or her technical or professional abilities. If these are clearly demonstrated and some evidence of leadership capability shown, the individual is eventually promoted to position A2. At this point he or she should delegate some of the professional or technical work (Do) to subordinates and take on additional (Direct) duties. In the case of the factory supervisor, this first transition is easier because from the beginning of the assignment, the Do aspect is almost automatically eliminated by the union contract and there is a clear and distinct shift to the Direct mode along with a reassignment of organizational duties. But in most other instances, newly appointed managers find that they're still performing many aspects of their old job, with a few supervisory and administrative chores added on. Let's look at one newly appointed manager in particular. At this point either she sheds some of her technical or professional work or she starts getting further and further behind and begins to take work home or stay in the office after closing time—*dangerous precedents!*

"Now let's say that she succeeds in keeping on top of her assignment, and she receives additional promotions to point A3 on the chart. You can see that now the administrative side of her work is making even greater demands on her time. In order to keep up with her most vital responsibility (that aspect which differentiates jobs on the managerial hierarchy and justifies a salary increase), either she has to spin off nearly all of her technical and professional work or she cuts even more into her nonwork time. Now in order to reduce substantially the professional and technical side of her work activities, she would have to make a major change in her *modus operandi*. But she's not likely to change what she feels has been largely responsible for her successful rise through the ranks. Instead, she gets a second filing cabinet and a larger briefcase to store the work she must get to when she can find a spare moment.

"Her work day is filled with technical and professional activities of her own and fragmented by interruptions of a similar nature from subordinates, with the inevitable result that those aspects of her job which can be put off—usually the uniquely managerial tasks of planning and organizing—are postponed and addressed with diminished energies at the end of a frantic day. Of course she can and often does cut into her weekends which she so desperately needs for herself and perhaps a family, but doing this repeatedly risks damaging her home life, not to mention her golf score.

"As she gets further and further into the hole, she simply doesn't seem to have the time to find a way to get out of it. She's frantic at work, exhausted at home, and she knows deep in her heart that she's not doing the kind of job she hoped she would, and she's really not getting any fun out of life either. Crazy, isn't it?"

MacCallum's making sense, I thought to myself. It's almost always the critical work demanding my closest attention and concentration that finds its way into my briefcase to be done at home, often when I'm least in the mood to tackle tasks that require my greatest powers of insight and creativity. He's right, I often just don't seem to have the time to deal adequately with the parts of my job that in theory differentiate it from my previous position. . . . But here my reverie was interrupted by MacCallum.

"But even if our manager does delegate some of her technical and professional work, her natural tendency

is to pass on only the routine aspects of her former job—
the ones she really disliked doing—without regard for
the effect that this is likely to have on the job satisfaction of the recipients. And as if this were not enough, she
all too often gives very precise instructions as to how
she wants each task to be performed, effectively elimi-
nating any satisfaction that might result from problem
solving and method determination. This has a whole
spectrum of outcomes. From the point of view of the
superior it's quite natural to want to get rid of the less-
satisfying parts of her old assignment as well as to ensure that they be done competently by giving precise,
step-by-step direction—after all, who could be better
qualified to determine the best methods than the seasoned veteran? But this practice of emphasizing the
'how to do it' aspects has other repercussions: it often
spreads out to include new tasks never undertaken by
the boss herself and thus the problem-solving and
method-determination aspects of her work increase the
demands on her to the point that the time she saved by
delegating some of the routine professional aspects of
her work is more than offset by a new order of technical
activity. Under these conditions delegation does not
free the work time needed for higher-level managerial
tasks."

"Can you spell that out for me?" I asked.

"OK, let me give you an example," he replied. "Al was
vice president in charge of purchasing when I was a
clerk in the automobile company where I began my industrial career. He had been a buyer before he took over
the entire purchasing function, and he had a tremen-
dously capable staff working for him. Al used to spend
his entire workday talking to his direct subordinates
one after the other, checking with them on their 'open to
buy positions' and their inventory of crucial parts that

could close down the final assembly line. If he found any problems in the course of this checkup (as he always did) he'd either deal with the problems himself, usually not as effectively as the buyer involved who had built up a superb relationship with the vendors, or he'd give detailed instructions for treating the matter at hand, making it clear that the buyer was to consult him before taking any action that deviated from those instructions. Only after the buyers had gone home did he take on the duties of a vice president, having spent what should have been the most productive time of the day, when his mind was at its freshest, doing his subordinates' work for them. He'd wind up going home at night with a briefcase full of the work he was really paid to do. Instead of seeing himself as a vice president with responsibility for the purchasing function, he behaved like a senior super buyer more involved with the process of purchasing than with the relationship of this function to corporate welfare or survival. Maybe if Al had been less of a perfectionist as a buyer, he'd have been a lot better as a corporate executive. In a word, he just wouldn't give up the structured activities he knew and loved to take on a qualitatively different perspective. You see, from his point of view, each promotion he'd received brought with it a quantitative increase rather than a qualitative change in his responsibilities—he didn't see each step as an opportunity to develop a broader perspective which could ultimately lead to an executive vice presidency, or even the presidency of the organization. He should have been constantly appraising the relationships between purchasing and the other departments in the company, as well as his functional responsibility. He should have also been monitoring changes in the social and economic environment, and their impact on the corporation. Al also should have been developing a range of options to deal with these new developments, since this range is usually much wider if change is anticipated rather than reacted to when it ultimately presents itself as a full-blown crisis. But since poor Al was never able to function as an executive, he remained a technician, and in spite of the jammed briefcase he took home every night, he shamefully neglected the activities that justified his high salary. He never really organized himself or his department and accordingly short-changed the company and himself."

MacCallum's line of reasoning sounded convincing, so I probed further. "What about the subordinates under these conditions? You said that they're often deprived of the job satisfaction that comes from problem-solving achievements in carrying out their assignments."

"Two possibilities," said MacCallum. "The good ones—the ones Flowers and Hughes call 'turn ons'[5]—nearly always have other employment options, and they tend to leave after they find out this is the way things are done and that they're hewers of wood and drawers of water rather than real professionals in the eyes of their boss. The others, the 'turn offs,' soon realize that their superior still likes to show his technical competence; it makes the boss feel good, and besides, if the method he suggests doesn't work out, then he's partly to blame. It's a win/win situation, so pretty soon they come to him asking for a solution to every technical problem. He obliges; they become truly dependent on him, a child/parent relationship if you like, and after a while they can't function without him. All of this slows their development enormously and results in incredible demands on the boss's time, limiting even further his ability to function at a higher level. It's a vicious circle, and once managers get caught in it, breaking out is extremely difficult."

"A matter of habit," I commented.

"That's only a partial explanation. I think there are at least two other reasons that are even more significant. First, as I pointed out, problems are challenging and fun, and bosses, though they may not admit this, often enjoy them. This is particularly true if they're engineers; engineers usually relish technical problems and are often anxious to prove to themselves and to their subordinates that they're every inch the engineers they ever were. Second, they really aren't sure of what they should be doing as managers and they're even less sure of how they should go about doing it. They haven't taken the time to really think about the nature of their jobs as opposed to their old technical assignments with additional supervisory responsibility. Like all of us; no, I mean all of *you*. *I* don't feel this way any more. *You* all pride yourselves on being busy and working ferociously hard. In fact your bragging goes something like this: 'God, I am busy. The phone rings every two minutes; my subordinates keep coming to me with problems rather than solutions; I never get a chance to think about what I'm doing. It's just one big scramble—a mad rat race!' The whole lot of you should be called 'busynesspeople' rather than managers. You prefer the structured activity that's the prerequisite for a more ordered life as a manager. Like mine, for example."

"How did you work your way out of the rat race?" I asked. He sounded so infuriatingly smug, but maybe, just maybe, he had something I could use.

"When I first became manager of a small refinery," he said, "I took care not to neglect the executive and administrative aspects of my assignment, and by making massive intrusions into my nonwork time, I was promoted to my present position in a much larger operation. As soon as I started to think about how much more responsibility I was taking on, I realized I'd go out of my mind if I tried to continue to do it the same old way, reducing my nonbusiness time even further, so I decided to do something about it. If you let it, work will drive out everything else, golf included."

"So what did you do?" I asked. This whole scenario was beginning to sound more and more familiar. I'd seen this happening to me over a period of time, but hadn't been able to do anything about it.

"The first step," said MacCallum, "was to take some time to really think about my job as a manager—I talked my boss into letting me take a week off just to think about my new assignment, nothing else.

"You know," he mused, "when you get right down to it, it's almost impossible to get any real thinking done at work. Not just because of interruptions, but almost more importantly, the whole psychological and physical environment in which managers work tends to discourage contemplation and encourage activity. The higher the level in an organization, the more critical is the role of reflection and the less important that of activity, but so often we've become conditioned on the way up through the organizational ranks. How many bosses would give a word of encouragement to a subordinate if they were to come upon him sitting at his desk, chair tipped back, foot resting on an open drawer, and staring into space with an abstract expression on his face? They'd be far more likely to ask him what the hell he's doing, and if the unfortunate replied, 'Thinking,' he'd probably be advised to stop thinking and get back to work. My daughter's studying to be a teacher, and she gave me a book by Jerome Bruner to read.[6] He mentions the symbolism of the right hand and the left, the one the doer and the other the dreamer, and it seems to me that for most managers, their extensive use of the right hand for doing provides little or no opportunity for the development of the left hand for dreaming, for the creative speculation associated with planning and organizing.

"Contemplating one's job and how best to perform it is much less common than simply looking around and seeing how others perform similar assignments. But then I wanted to save my imperiled golf game," he continued, "so that was the first essential step, and I took it."

"OK, but did you have a positive model in developing your system?" I asked, thinking to myself that he couldn't have worked it out totally by himself in one week or while he was running a refinery.

"Yes, as a matter of fact I did," he admitted with a half-smile, "probably the most effective manager I've ever met and he wasn't even in manufacturing. Let me tell you about him. A few years ago I was asked to a party at a neighbor's house to celebrate Bob's promotion to an assistant secretary's position at an insurance company. I was impressed and congratulated him on his appointment. He shrugged it off with the comment that insurance companies have as many assistant secretaries as a hound dog has fleas, but he did admit that he was pleased with the recognition. A short time afterwards Bob moved out of the neighborhood, and I lost touch with him for a couple of years. Then I ran into him at a cocktail party and naturally asked if he was still with the same company. He said he was, but in a different capacity—he was now an executive vice president. Remembering his comment on his last promotion I asked if insurance companies have as many executive vice presidents as the proverbial dog has fleas. Bob's

response was that he was one of two line officers reporting to the president. Not bad for a man in his forties, I
thought, so I asked him what I thought was a central
question, even though I'm not sure I expected an answer:

"Can you identify any key decision you made during
your managerial career that you feel particularly affected your success in the company?"

"That's a hard question," he replied, but he gave me
an answer, and as well as I can remember, it went like
this:

"Basically there are two main routes to the top of a
casualty company like ours: marketing and underwriting. When I started work I chose the underwriting side.
Let me tell you right now that I was, and still am, quite
an underwriter, partly because I really like it. Anyway, I
did the job so well that before long I was promoted to
supervising underwriter. After two years I was transferred back to the head office and given additional responsibilities, supervising a greater number of underwriters, but still doing some of the technical work
myself. In other words, the job was pretty much the
same in content, but its scope had increased. Gradually
I became aware of another difference—the chaotic nature of my work day. When I thought about the reasons,
it struck me that I was spending too much time telling
people how to do their jobs rather than emphasizing
what had to be done. Perhaps because of my own fasci-
nation with the process of underwriting, I was concen-
trating on *method* rather than *output*. So I made an effort to stop doing this; actually I cut down drastically
on giving technical advice and spent more time working
out what I expected from my subordinates in terms of
production and letting them know what organizational
resources, including limited amounts of my time, were

available to help them with problems they encountered. In addition I designed a control system to keep them and me informed of the quality and the quantity of their output. This was critical; to be effective, such a system must be precise, timely, and trusted by everyone involved. That was no small order, but I felt the time spent designing such a control mechanism would pay off handsomely for my subordinates, myself, and of course, for the organization.

"At this stage of my managerial career, it was becoming increasingly clear to me that my job was largely one of getting commitment to organizational objectives and monitoring the output of my subordinates. Now let me make one point clear: to get real commitment to my goals, and not just verbal agreement, required time to explore differences in opinion and perception. In any hierarchy it's easy for a superior to confuse surface agreement reluctantly given under implicit pressure and with unarticulated reservations by a docile and somewhat intimidated subordinate with *real* commitment between two mature people negotiating, to the extent possible, as equals—and believe me this takes *skill* as well as *time* on the part of the superior. For me to have this kind of time I had to make sure that almost all the problems encountered by the underwriters would be solved at lower organizational levels and not passed up to me. Here I simply refused to answer questions on process problems, referring the asker of one of several subordinates whom I had designated as official problem-solvers and, in the case of particularly difficult situations, requesting a post facto report on how it was handled. Along with my control mechanism, this approach let me assess accurately the capabilities of my key, most promotable subordinates. I really had this system working well when I was transferred out to the field again—this time as an assistant branch manager—which is when I made my key decision. In a word, the decision was no more underwriting, for that was no longer what I was paid to do. My new assignment was not to perform technical tasks, but to design and manage a system to ensure that responsibilities for underwriting as well as those for marketing, accounting, personnel, and so on, were being carried out as effectively as possible.

"You know, the higher you go in an organization, the more impossible it becomes to understand the technical aspects of your subordinates' jobs. And the more important becomes the administrative skill of negotiating and gaining commitment to sets of performance objectives for maximal organizational effectiveness. So with few exceptions, I refused to get involved in problem solving. This was much easier in those parts of the business where I had only limited expertise than it was in my own field—underwriting—but I managed to do it even there. I realized I had to stop doing my subordinates' work for them, no matter how intriguing it might be, so that I could concentrate on my own responsibilities.

"Once I did this successfully, I not only had the time I needed to negotiate outputs with my subordinates, but even more important, I had the time to plan, to reflect on developments within and outside the branch that seemed likely to affect us and to develop a variety of approaches to deal with them before they reached critical stages. You know, managerial planning is often mistaken for brilliance and successful management for single-minded devotion to duty, and because I was seen as brilliant and dedicated, the president couldn't wait to promote me to a position where he had direct access to my capabilities.

"So now you know the truth," MacCallum concluded,

"I didn't develop the system on my own; I adapted Bob's to my situation, and you can too!"

I have known lots of Als in my management career but very few Bobs, who were able to avoid or even downplay their involvement in the technical aspect of their subordinates' work in order to concentrate on administration and planning.

"Let's get back to you. You say negotiating outputs with subordinates, designing a control system scanning the environment, and preparing contingency plans are the essential middle- and upper-level managerial responsibilities. Can you be more specific in your own case?" I asked.

"OK, first let's look at the process of negotiating with subordinates. It takes a lot of time, but the payoff in terms of commitment is tremendous. Many times an individual insists at the outset that he or she is only capable of attaining unrealistically low performance targets, which practically guarantees success. In these instances it's necessary to point out that others with similar assignments are doing more and to suggest that he or she discuss methods and approaches with specifically identified people. On the other hand, an unduly optimistic subordinate may suggest objectives that are obviously too high. In this situation, to retain the effectiveness of the whole process, I point out that while I would be delighted if they were reached I would still be satisfied with a lower level of accomplishment. Finally, because of changes in the environment which are beyond the subordinate's control—changes in the level of consumer demand for example—the level of 'output' must be periodically renegotiated to retain that commitment. As Bob warned, this does take a lot of time.

"Now let's look at organization design. This whole approach requires that managerial jobs be set up and maintained in terms of output rather than process, and it requires a shift in focus from the traditional managerial concern with activities to an emphasis on results.[7] As I said before, the design and monitoring of a reporting system are necessary so that *both* of you are confident that you are constantly informed of the effectiveness of the operation. Don't underestimate the effort and time that system design requires. It often takes real imagination and creativity to define certain jobs in terms of output, and there's an almost irresistible temptation to skip the difficult ones and say that they can't be reduced to these terms. One approach I've found useful in these instances is to ask myself how I know the task is being competently performed at all, and then go on from there.

"Finally and perhaps most important, I continually monitor the environment in which I operate my total unit. By this I mean I constantly watch all those developments, technical and economic, that are likely to affect operations. I make the necessary adjustments to enable my unit to adapt creatively, taking advantage of opportunities and mitigating threats at an early stage. To do this I need blocks of time for thinking, which is only possible with competent, highly motivated subordinates and the confidence that my control system will let us both know that output is deviating from standard in time to take corrective actions before critical situations develop.

"As I see it, this is the essence of management at the highest levels of any organization: bringing its strategy and structure[8] into line with a constantly changing and developing environment and the threats and opportunities that it provides. But this approach can only be implemented if managers use their time to do those things for which they are being paid that financial premium over their subordinates. If they are foolish enough to try to do the subordinates' work with its typically greater emphasis on technique and process, either they will neglect their higher responsibilities, or they will sacrifice their nonwork time or both. And, it is so easy for this to happen that before long they have established the *modus operandi* for most of the organization's managers."

"OK, after you thought out your managerial responsibilities step by step, how did you go about setting up your systems and how do you use your time?" I asked. I had to have answers to those questions before the plane landed and I was back in my frantic world of short work periods punctuated by what I was sure MacCallum would have viewed as unnecessary and inappropriate interruptions.

"I'll try to answer your questions one at a time," he replied, "but they run into each other. It all began with competent motivated subordinates, as I said before, but at the outset I didn't know which of my people really fit into that category. Sure I had some ideas, but when I started to think about it, I wasn't all that confident as to how competent each of them really was. I guess, like a lot of managers, I had impressions, some of them no doubt more accurate than others. I certainly had *some* hard data on their performance, but when it came down to an accurate assessment of their capability and potential—we have to evaluate our people once a year—I wasn't too sure that I hadn't introduced at least two errors into my appraisals in the past. The obvious one was a kind of personality 'halo effect.' I tended to rate highly those people whose personalities I found pleasing, people who held my own views, prejudices, and values. The second error was that I did the same for those who readily took my advice—those who had been able to pass on to me the more difficult decision-making requirements of their jobs, increasing *my* job demands, and as I mentioned before, taking my time away from things *I* should be doing—usually planning—or things *I* wanted to do—usually golf. I had to start somewhere, so as much as I could, I refused to help my subordinates make operating decisions; in fact, I began scheduling a weekly Thursday meeting during which my seven subordinates told me about the decisions they made during the past seven days and if they received help, who helped them. Like Bob, I began trying to refuse to be seduced into doing their technical work for them."

"Wait a minute," I interrupted, "suppose subordinates simply do not know how to approach a problem. What then?"

"Well, at the outset, I lead them through the decision process by asking them to tell me the options they have in dealing with the problem, one by one, and then speculate on the most likely outcomes of each—sort of a modified Socratic approach. Most often they have the technical expertise and judgment to deal with the situations, but they lack the necessary self-confidence or have become accustomed to passing on the tough problems to their superiors. Gradually I start to refer them to their peers for help with problems they can't handle themselves and then ask them to tell me how they have worked them out. After a while a pattern develops, and they seem to refer with increasing regularity to one or two individuals. Eventually I let one of these regular problem solvers take over the Thursday meetings when I was out of the office.

"When they report their decisions at the Thursday meeting, my subordinates have to give credit to whoever has helped them, at least if they want further help from that quarter in the future. Besides, each subordinate is anxious to help his or her counterparts because of the recognition at the meeting. My subordinates soon find out who is the most capable and helpful among them, and these in turn become candidates for the Thursday chair assignment. These are also the people I recommend for promotion when jobs as refinery managers open up in the corporation—so it's a job they compete for among themselves, by being as helpful to their peers and as competent as they can. After a while the Thursday chair becomes the specialist of last resort. After all, my subordinates are at least as technically capable as I am, and in many cases more so. I'm a member of the slide-rule generation, and I only learned the computer later on, while they were raised on it. It's so much better for them to solve their own problems and to develop their skills than to rely on mine and to hedge the risks inherent in technical decision making."

"What do you do if during the course of a Thursday meeting a subordinate reports on a decision that seems to you to be a mistake? Do you overrule it?" I asked.

"That depends on how much the mistake is likely to cost and how sure I am that it really is an error. The benefits to an organization of *real* decentralized decision making are great: quicker decisions at the operating site, training and experience for the decision maker—which brings with it the challenge, growth, recognition, and advancement Herzberg says result in motivation[9] and of course greater freedom from interruption at upper levels of management."

"Sounds a bit risky to me," I commented.

"Sure it has its risk side, and of course, that's the risk of mistakes. If a subordinate reports a decision at a Thursday meeting that I'm pretty sure is an error and is likely to cost us some money, say five or six hundred dollars and if the individual involved has not made many mistakes in the past, I often feel it would be a worthwhile learning experience for that person, one which could be worth more to the company than the potential loss, so I may well let him or her make it and face up to the consequences. If the amount of potential loss is more substantial or if the decision maker has been responsible for several errors in judgment in the recent past, I often question the decision by suggesting possible outcomes of the proposed course of action. Sometimes others at the meeting, often the Thursday chair, do this on their own. Or I may suggest that the group discuss the issue in more detail. Seldom do I actually have to overrule operating decisions though; usually the decision maker comes through. Individuals do learn by making mistakes, and they have to be free to make minor ones if they are to develop as managers."

"You mentioned that besides designing the managerial system, executives must also monitor their operations. The Thursday meeting is clearly after the fact," I observed.

"True, but it's not just the superior who needs this information—the subordinate needs it, and not only to monitor operations and to make appropriate adjustments. As Lawler and Hackman[10] put it, four factors substantially affect job satisfaction: there's variety, autonomy, and task identity—and the nature of my subordinates' assignments certainly pay attention to these aspects, but they need the fourth component to complete the set, feedback from the job itself. Obviously I need it for control purposes; otherwise I could not leave them to make their own decisions and still be able to sleep at night, or to sink those long putts," he added with a smile.

"When I took over the refinery I'm running now," he continued, "or more accurately, that my subordinates are running, I spent a lot of time designing a control system, one in which I had complete confidence, so that I would not have to make continual phone calls and inspection tours. I once read something to the effect that control is the adjustment of operations to predetermined standards and that its basis is information in the hands of the manager.[11] Well I know that to get real commitment, these standards would have to be negotiated and accepted by the individual responsible for making the appropriate adjustments *before* not *after* critical situations and, like Harold Geneen at ITT, I hate surprises. I worked with our computer people on how we could get information on the outputs we had negotiated in time for corrective actions to be taken so that our entire unit could reach its operating objectives within the target periods. I didn't want to be the relayer of this data because I don't like being put in the role of some kind of policeman. Nor do I want to be involved in the solution of someone else's problems, least of all those my subordinates are being paid to solve. So we worked out a system such that they receive up-to-the-minute production, quality, and cost data on Wednesday noon—our production week ends on Friday night—and I receive it late Wednesday afternoon. This accomplishes two things. First, they have time to make adjustments to their operations before the end of the production week so that we meet our schedule. Second, they can work out their approaches to the problems before I receive the data, and when they call me, they tell me how they are going to deal with the problem situations rather than asking me what they should do. If their approaches are sound, I let them go ahead; if not, I tell them to work on them some more."

"Two questions," I interposed, "suppose at this point the subordinate still cannot work out the solution, would you help? Second, if you're not directly involved in engineering any more, how do you know whether the proposals are sound?"

"Well," he replied, "I probably still wouldn't get involved in a subordinate's operating problems. Most likely I'd refer him or her to a colleague, or if it were a very difficult situation I'd suggest pretty strongly taking it up with the Thursday chair and let me know how they were going to deal with the problem. As for no longer being involved in engineering, I should explain that with my management system I now have time to keep up with my technical reading, and I'm very much involved in engineering. I simply refuse to use my knowledge to solve problems other people are being paid to solve. When they do solve them themselves, they're more likely to try and implement them as effectively as possible. Besides, I need this technical knowledge for the other aspects of my work."

"What are those?" I asked.

"Primarily anticipating changes in my operations resulting from shifts in demand or from developments in technology. At the moment I have manning and equipment tables for my refinery instantly available in my office at six possible levels of output. I've also worked out the sequence for adding additional resources to achieve this production in one, three, or five years. Technology changes rapidly in the oil business, and I have to spend quite a bit of time developing these data."

"Do any of your subordinates help you with this part of your job?" I queried.

"Yes and no. I don't let them take part in the final stages of planning for two reasons: first, if the projections work out well I want to take all the credit; second, if they're wrong, I'm the only one who can take the blame. I do use the Thursday chair to help gather and sort out the information I need, and I also want that person to see how this aspect of a refinery manager's job is carried out. You see I lose my Thursday chair quite often—they get promoted to my position in smaller units with amazing regularity. My refinery is getting quite a reputation as a training ground for refinery managers, and I have no trouble getting first-class subordinates—capable people want and seek the opportunity to operate their units with minimal interference from above, and they soon find out that promotion at our refinery is based as much on their skill in working with their peers as it is on their technical expertise.

"You know, I suppose it's to be expected, but this whole approach is working its way down through the organization. I understand that subordinates are holding regular meetings with their supervisors and have set up minicontrol systems based on cost information and negotiation of standards—not unlike Scheid's charter of accountability for executives.[12] I'm even seeing evidence that my subordinates are beginning to anticipate problems and opportunities rather than merely reacting to them."

Our plane came to a complete stop at the terminal gate, and MacCallum stood up and moved toward the aisle. As he waved goodbye he said, "I'll be thinking about you hard at work when I start out on the tournament tomorrow."

"Damn you, MacCallum," I muttered to myself after I greeted my wife at the airport.

"What's that, dear?" she asked.

"Oh, nothing. I was just thinking that tomorrow I've got to get really organized."

MACCORMICK

*Whatever Happened to the American
Managerial Revolution?*

. . . Maybe MBO?

NO DOUBT about it, he looked distinguished:
over six feet tall and gray haired, wearing an
immaculately tailored suit that emphasized his trim
figure, he studied the classified ads in the *International
Herald Tribune* intently. We were sitting side by side in
the departure lounge of the TWA building at JFK await-
ing the boarding announcement for the evening flight to
London. He glanced up at the clouds and then over at
me and said casually, "I wonder whether we'll arrive on
schedule this trip, although for the first time in years it
really doesn't matter to me too much. What about you,
are you on a tight schedule?"

"Kind of. I'd like to see a bit of London again before I
take the night flight to Hanover tomorrow," I replied.
"I'm on the way to the trade show to check on some new
German and Japanese machine tools for my machine
shop in Ohio, so I guess I'd be disappointed if we were
late, but TWA has been pretty good in the past. How
about you? If you're not really worried about schedules,
this must be a pleasure trip."

"Yes it is—I retired last week after twenty-eight years

as a management consultant, and I'm going back to Britain to see if it's practical to buy a small house in the Cotswolds where my wife and I can spend part of the year. A boyhood dream I guess, but it may not be practical. We'll just have to see."

"You say 'back to Britain,' but your Boston accent tells me you've been in this country for some time. When did you come to the States and why, if I may ask, when you had the Cotswold dream?"

"I was an engineering officer in the Royal Navy during the war, and when I was demobilized I wasn't interested in going back to my old job at the Rover works near Birmingham," he explained. "I'd had enough of boilers and turbines, and I had no desire to go back to designing axles and power trains. I thought that management might offer more of what interested me. In the mid-forties the U.S. seemed to be the place to go to learn about management, so I came here, finished an MBA, got intrigued, and hung on for the PhD. I did a stint as an assistant professor in the southwest, but found it all a bit unreal in terms of the world as I knew and remembered it and longed to get back to real problems in an industrial setting. Since PhDs in business with an engineering background and industrial experience were as scarce as hen's teeth, I got a job with a prestigious consulting outfit, worked my way up to principal after a while, and stayed on in a variety of assignments. But enough about me—you've extracted my life story. Name is MacCormick. How about you?"

"Fred Riter here. My story's not nearly as interesting as yours. I graduated from business school just after World War II, took a job with a major U.S. manufacturer in the electrical industry, ended up in the production side, and came to feel I had reached a plateau. I was clearly slated for my boss's job when he was four long years away from retirement, but I heard about a job in a small, growing, parts manufacturing company in Ohio. What intrigued me was the opportunity not just to make major executive decisions about the company's future directions and authorize the necessary capital commitments, but also to build up my own equity in the firm. I made more good decisions than bad ones—my boss retired five years ago, and while the old gentleman is still on the board of directors, I'm the CEO, own a fair chunk of the action, and run my seventy-five-employee operation near Toledo. That's about all there is to it." By this time MacCormick's expression was one of concentration and concern. He seemed to be a good listener, and his background, experience, and different perspective promised good conversation about a common concern: effective management.

"You pointed out that you came to this country from Europe thirty-five years ago to learn about management," I continued. "Well, even though I'd prefer to make what for us is a heavy investment in capital goods in the U.S., I'm on my way to Europe now because I've concluded that I'll get better value and financial return if I buy Japanese or German equipment. And unless I'm mistaken, that suggests either we've lost our managerial leadership or we're well on the way to losing it. Certainly we can't hide behind the notion that our total labor costs are substantially higher than theirs—that's simply not true any longer. You've been involved in this situation as it's developed; do you think I'm imagining things, or are we losing our touch?" I asked, thinking to myself that a sometime college professor and consultant like MacCormick would love to talk—and would have lots to say on this controversial and very real topic. As I sat back, MacCormick jumped right in.

"I have to confess I'm glad you asked that question,

because I've been thinking about it a great deal in the last couple of years. Many of my clients have been focusing on the whole question of the role of management, not only in increasing industrial productivity, but also in improving the efficiency with which social services, in the fullest sense of the word, are delivered. Recently, in fact, I ran across the reprint of a speech by a Professor Litterer in which he referred to 'Management as a Social Necessity'[1]—acknowledging, if you will, the multidimensional impact of this essential activity. But before I can answer your question, I have to go over a bit of history."

For a minute, I was afraid that MacCormick the college professor was going to take over, but his next words reassured me.

"I'll skip over the emergence of the managerial function in the building of pyramids, the role of Moses in the exodus from Egypt, and even management in the industrial revolution in Britain and ultimately in the U.S. The first *really* influential school of managerial thinkers and practitioners concentrated on the mechanical aspects or more specifically, the industrial engineering aspects of the managerial task. Frederick W. Taylor's *Scientific Management*[2] (which, incidentally, is not as cold-blooded in its approach to people as many believe it to be) had a profound influence on how managers went about their jobs. As you may know, Gannt with his precise charts followed Taylor, as did Gilbreth with time-and-motion studies and some interest in the human dimension. There were others, of course, who took a primarily mechanistic approach, including Fayol with his view from the top of the organization and his emphasis on the uniquely managerial responsibilities of planning, organizing, commanding, and controlling. This kind of emphasis on how tasks should be performed and how they should relate to each other finds modern expression in systems theory, which has received such a boost from the advent and ultimate, though in many cases reluctant, acceptance of the computer as an essential managerial tool. I think you could even say that Fayol's top management point of view is carried on and greatly developed by Peter Drucker."

"How about the behaviorists, aren't you neglecting them?" I asked, anxious to get in a few words edgewise.

"Right. Mayo, McGregor, and that lot turned managers' attention to the human aspects of effective rather than merely efficient management, the difference being the additional element of motivation to be achieved by the personal commitment of the worker. This school also has many contemporary heirs, like Herzberg, Porter, Blauner Haire, and so on. Then too, I suppose you could say the organizational theory bunch draws heavily on the applied behaviorists."

"Can you name some firms that have come close to applying the mechanistic and behavioral theories you mentioned?" I asked, hoping to lead MacCormick out of the classroom and back to reality.

"Well, I'll take a stab at it," he said. "On the mechanical side, I'd point to the pure conglomerates like Textron and ITT. These were really put together for financial rather than synergistic reasons—even if this was the reason given when the merger or takeover occurred. A second class of this type might be mature companies in mature industries, like GM or GE. As for the behavioral, maybe newer organizations, particularly those with an emphasis on higher technology, whose survival depends on creativity—possibly Polaroid or Texas Instruments. But keep in mind that these are just my impressions; I can't really cite particular companies on the basis of systematic observation and careful analysis, and I can think of many exceptions even in the cases I've mentioned. For example, I'd expect to find a higher degree of sensitivity to the necessary behavioral ingredients to maintain a creative atmosphere in the labs at the GM Technical Center than I would at a GMAD assembly plant, but even at Polaroid I'd expect to find the same sort of thing. And there are other factors operating too: by no means is all managerial behavior institutionally determined, because the beliefs and value structure of the individual manager are so influential in establishing the work atmosphere for his or her subordinates. In micro terms, when we move in on individual managers, they're operating on several levels, and the extent to which their jobs have components that are technical, strategy formulating, and enabling, rather than directing affects the environment in which subordinates function. In *The Meanings of Management*,[3] David Reed identifies three roles for managers: the technician, the scientific manager (the leader with primarily human relations or behavioral responsibility), and finally the trustee (with an emphasis on adjusting operations to changing external factors within both the organization and the larger economic environment). Anyway, I suppose all this has led to the recent interest academics are showing in the contingency approach to management. Really, they're just giving official acknowledgment to what many effective practicing managers have always known: that in choosing the optimal method for carrying out managerial responsibilities, *It All Depends*, to cite the name of a book advocating this approach.[4] But let's get back to the broader questions. . . ."

Yes, let's, I muttered to myself and interjected, "I guess what really interests me though, is whatever happened to the 'management revolution' in the U.S.? So much of its development occurred here, yet we seem to have lost our leadership."

"I was getting to that," he flashed back somewhat

brusquely. "Somewhere along the line, exactly when I don't know, a new school developed. It may have been an unconscious attempt to achieve a synthesis between the scientific managers with their emphasis on how to do the task with utmost efficiency and the applied behaviorists with their emphasis on motivation and commitment. In any case, the main exponents of this school included Peter Drucker, whom I mentioned earlier, and George Odiorne, both of whom did much to operationalize the concept of management by objectives (MBO).[5] In its present form MBO draws on the mechanical approach, specifically systems theory with its emphasis on outputs and control, as well as on behavioral theory with its stress on the motivational payoff that comes from gaining the commitment of the individuals responsible for providing the inputs."

"Nothing wrong there," I commented. "Managers have been doing that for years. Maybe they've often settled for a skillful sales job laid on their subordinates instead of negotiations, but still. . . . And besides, control is what management is all about. I don't see anything wrong with MBO."

"Neither do I," he assured me. "In fact, I'm a real advocate. A lot of my consulting work has involved designing and installing MBO programs for a variety of companies and not-for-profit institutions, and I've made a lot of money out of it! As you say, who can argue with the idea of having the superior and the subordinate sit down together at regular intervals during the year to work out innovative, problem solving, and routine objectives, and their criteria for appraising performance in relation to these objectives at the next scheduled review session? It's so logical, and besides, your comment that it merely institutionalizes what many effective managers have been doing for years is quite true.

As I see it, the villain in the piece doesn't lurk in the concept of MBO, but in its application. No, not just the application, but also the current climate existing in many U.S. firms where this approach to management is used."

"Can you be a bit more specific as to how this has affected the competitive ability of U.S. firms?" I was really having trouble nailing MacCormick down. "It seems to me that the competitive ability of a firm results from the combined contribution of its workers, managers, and shareholders, but I suppose the key factor is management. Anyway, what happened to the American management revolution?"

"Slow down. Don't rush me," said McCormick testily. "That's the trouble with all you managers, and Americans are the worst, I might add. You ask a complex question, and you want a simple answer in ten words or less. OK, let's look at the three groups you mentioned. Only I'm going to split managers into two: those up to and including middle-level and those on the top. But let's start with the first group you cited, the workers.

"Most, but not all, workers in major U.S. firms are unionized, for whatever reasons you choose to give. I suppose this factor, combined with the history and nature of U.S. unions, has reduced the commitment of the American workers to their company. I have no first-hand experience with Japanese management, but from what I've read about workers' job attitudes and from the few Japanese managers I've talked to, I'm not surprised that Japan has taken over as the number one world producer of motor vehicles. True, there are other factors at work too, and I'll mention a few of these later, but let's start with the U.S. workers. By and large I have the impression that in many, if not most, firms (fortunately, by no means all) managers see workers as a factor of production, and an expensive one at that. The devastating economic and personal consequences of economic plant shutdowns have led unions in the U.S. to argue for the concept of job ownership rights. Admittedly this contrasts with the more people-centered view of firms like Johnson & Johnson or Eastman Kodak, but only too often when the role of workers is mentioned at all by top management, it's to remind them of foreign competition, with the implication that they have to work harder or better."[6]

"But you did mention several exceptions to this pattern of limited organizational attention to individual workers' contributions and subsequent value to the corporation," I pointed out. "Do these firms have anything in common? Do they fall into any definite categories?" Damn it, MacCormick, I thought to myself, I happen to make one hell of an effort to encourage my workers to contribute suggestions and ideas, not only to improve our competitive position, but also to make it a better place to work. And I think this has helped us stop a couple of half-hearted attempts to unionize our workers.

"That's a toughie," MacCormick admitted. "I've given this a lot of thought too, and I think I can identify three general classes of firms, although there may well be more. First, some firms that, either through patent protection, skilled management, or both, have achieved unusually high levels of market penetration and attribute at least some of their success to enlightened personnel policies and the effect these policies have in gaining support from their workers. I suppose Eastman Kodak and Johnson & Johnson, which I mentioned earlier, might fit here. Second, the high-technology group which depends heavily on creative contributions from employees for their success in the marketplace, maybe

Texas Instrument or Polaroid. I mentioned both of these earlier too. It seems as though we're developing a pattern here, doesn't it? Third, I think there is this tendency in firms where managers exercise a considerable degree of financial control over their enterprises, like Michelin, for example, and in smaller ones, maybe like yours, where ownership and management are essentially the same. I'm not particularly happy with these categories, since they're not discrete, for one thing: there's a lot of overlapping. For another, I can think of exceptions, and finally, it's intuitive rather than scientifically based. But you did ask for my impressions, and that's what you got."

I was glad he included the last category. Small businesses like mine haven't got much going for them unless they do get more effort, a greater contribution, and more flexibility from their people than do most of the biggies. We're always in competition with them for some part of a market they don't want to dominate completely, at least not at the moment. Nowadays we have to pay essentially the same wages and benefits as the others, and given our limited clerical capacity, we're subject to what seems to me proportionately greater amounts of government harrassment. Besides, we haven't got the same ability to generate capital or to borrow it. We *have* to be ingenious and flexible—two key components which spell success for small businesses—and achieving this combination requires more sensitivity to and understanding of our workers than is the case for a corporate giant. . . .

Here MacCormick interrupted my musings.

"As I was saying, most workers, at least in production and some staff departments, including clericals, don't have much to say about the amount and nature of the output expected of them. Maybe an effort is made to sell them and their union on the fairness of the performance standard, but really that's about all.

"With the second category, organizational levels up to and including middle management, the picture gets a bit cloudier. In this group we run into real problems of definition from one company to another, but perhaps we can include here all managers except those at the very top, with responsibilities for determining organizational objectives, strategies, and policies. It's this group that has to maintain a capable group of producers whose output is consistent with organizational goals. So the impact of misguided and misinterpreted MBO is felt here first. Under MBO, theoretically at least, managers at all levels are supposed to provide input into the determination and establishment of their own performance objectives. But in my *experience*, this two-way process of performance targets establishment often doesn't get off the ground. First, given the realities of the organizational hierarchy, these objective-setting sessions usually degenerate to the point where the superior lays the output targets on the subordinate, who has little opportunity to meaningfully influence their determination, or else the meeting becomes a second-guessing exercise in which the subordinate manager attempts to discover what minimum performance objectives the boss will accept before they get put in writing. But that's not the only danger—there's another one operating in the opposite direction, namely that the subordinate, who finds the whole process uncomfortable or unreal given the unpredictability of the future, promises more than he or she can realistically hope to deliver in order to get the meeting over with quickly. In this case the subordinate's input is rapidly seized upon by a superior eager to have a new agreement, or even a better one suggested by the subordinate, as a means of pressing this hapless individual into greater effort. But in scenarios like this one, since the objective-setting superiors have just gone through the same procedure with their bosses, they really have very little jurisdiction over their subordinates' targets if they are to meet their own. I guess what I'm saying is that, as practiced in many if not most corporations, MBO has become a process of downward communication, and even downright pressure!"

"I remember working for a big corporation just after I graduated from college," I interjected, "where the cynics used to say that the formula for success was to keep moving every two years, horizontally if not vertically, so that your successor would be held responsible for your ambitious promises and plans."

"Uh huh," grunted MacCormick, clearly not amused. "Could be. You know this whole business isn't helped much by the current delusion top-level managers piously mouth to their immediate subordinates, namely that the latter are really the new entrepreneurial class and that they'll be expected to behave accordingly. Dr. Stanley Young,[7] an academic friend of mine, points out how absurd this notion really is, and as a small businessman who has observed the difficulties involved in capital formation and the isolation of almost totally independent decision making, you'd agree with him. All of this contributes to the breakdown of what was intended by the advocates of enlightened MBO, but the real problem lies at the top management level."

"I suppose most every aspect of organizational operations, good or bad, ultimately can be traced back to top management deficiencies or skills . . ." I began, but MacCormick interrupted.

"Yes, that's true enough—but let's go beyond the obvious. You recall, I commented earlier that two factors,

specifically the misapplication of MBO and the climate
in which it is applied in many U.S. firms, have resulted
in the declining ability of U.S. companies to compete
with foreign firms. Let me be a bit more specific. Top
management is concerned with controlling and maximizing performance, often in increasingly diversified
companies which lack a common product or even a
common market segment. Textron, for example, makes
and sells a line that includes fountain pens and helicop-
ters, and performance of its divisions can *only* be mea-
sured in financial terms. This is the *only* common denominator that can be applied to appraise the
management of its operating units and subsequently,
the top management of the corporation itself."

"Agreed, but what's wrong with that?" I asked. "The
raison d'être of any business large or small is to make a
profit, to maximize profit as I remember from my eco-
nomics courses. That's the way it is in a capitalist society...."

"True, true, but that doesn't go far enough," he shot
back. "The profit-maximization idea has been around
since long before the Cambridge economists dignified it
with their neat geometrical models, but what disturbs
me is that, partly thanks to misapplied MBO, it's
achieved new prominence and urgency eclipsing the
better Drucker notion that profit is the result of performing the managerial function well. I agree with his
view that the profit-maximization objective is extremely dangerous in the long run and with his sugges-
tion that making customers is a far better focus for organizational effort.[8] I'm with him on that, and you
probably are too. In the small businesses I've worked
with, managements have had to keep awfully close to
their customers' needs to survive...."

"We don't have much choice," I replied. "Too many

others want their business. I spend a lot of my time trying to figure out how to solve customers' production problems which they've been unable to deal with economically themselves. We simply have to be customer-oriented. But what's that got to do with MBO and short-term profit orientation?"

"Just this," he explained. "Increasingly, top-level managers are becoming short-run profit-oriented rather than customer- or even product-oriented. You know, Henry Ford probably liked money as much as the next person—certainly from all I've read he seemed to enjoy the power it brought—but he was also product-oriented. He liked cars per se, and he had a dream of putting America in wheels, a dream he certainly was responsible in part for achieving. Still, his company nearly collapsed in the face of competition from an organization that, soon after its founding, was far more finance centered than his product-based company: GM. Sure, GM focused on customer wants, recognized at the outset that a more attractive product could be offered with only slightly higher monthly payments, and even developed the annual model change and the idea of upgrading. But as an enterprise, it was essentially a financially oriented one with heavy emphasis on decentralized production and tight financial controls. Eventually Ford followed suit, particularly after GM-trained Ernie Breech took over. No question that financial controls are essential, but these days an emphasis on short-term profit measures, too often to the exclusion of virtually everything else, seems to be taking over in the U.S. . . . and when you add MBO—WOW! The long-run competitive ability of the organization is seriously impaired."

"Wait a minute," I interjected. "You're going too fast—I still don't see the connection."

"The whole focus of the organization changes when its orientation shifts from the production of goods aimed at satisfying a customer's real or latent need, which requires some degree of stimulation through advertising, to one of maximizing financial performance. Unfortunately, due to misapplied MBO, short-term financial results in so many U.S. firms are the sole manner by which the success of managers is judged and their appraisal and subsequent compensation is based almost totally on their units' return, on net assets and/or contribution to earnings. I could cite countless organizations where either this is a stated policy or where managers believe this to be the case and act accordingly, which naturally has exactly the same effect," he added.

"But why do you think what you refer to as misapplied MBO has affected this trend to appraise managerial performance in RONA and EPS terms? Personally I think they're pretty fair criteria to include as measures of effectiveness." Then I asked, "What do you mean by misapplied MBO anyway?"

"Misapplied MBO in my terminology means the reduction of the entire managerial appraisal process to a mere comparison of numbers: RONA and contribution to EPS in the case of the middle manager, short-run unit costs or equivalent for lower levels, either with a previously agreed upon list of targets or with results achieved by managers in other parts of the organization. This comes about, I believe, because financial results are readily quantifiable; they enable cross-organizational comparison and often, sadly enough, receive minimal interpretation; they're neat and clear and serve as the tools of an increasingly powerful group in the organization—the financial people. But that's another point I'll take up in a minute or two. I can see by the video screen up there that our departure has been delayed half an hour, so we have time.

"You see, properly applied MBO involves agreement between superior and subordinate on areas where managerial performance is critical for organizational effectiveness in the *long* run as well as the short run. Ideally, criteria for appraisal are included in the objective determination process, and the subordinate manager should provide input into the value to be placed on these measures. We've identified a couple of factors operating in many, if not most, MBO situations. I mentioned a moment ago that historical financial results are readily quantifiable. It's much harder to quantify criteria to appraise a manager's performance in innovating and hence building for the future (which all too soon becomes the past) performance of the operating unit. In addition, the superior manager is facing the same appraisal process and consequently is judged primarily, if not exclusively, using the same short-run financial criteria and so the pressure for financial results is passed on down through the management hierarchy. This pressure for optimal short-term performance is increased in large organizations where these criteria are used to rank individual managers in declining order, and it's common knowledge, or folklore—it really doesn't matter—that the bottom two or three on the list are likely to lose their jobs. So these twin objectives are pursued with what amounts to single-minded ferocity and potentially devastating long-term effects on the ability of the firm to compete against the Japanese and Europeans. De Lorean, in his *On a Clear Day You Can See General Motors*,[9] emphasizes the preoccupation of that much respected firm, in managerial terms at least, with short-run profits. Now he attributes this obsession in part to the increased control of consumer-goods companies by financial managers. I'd probably go even further than De Lorean and say that in firms not considered to be run by financial people, many top managers operate their companies primarily for short-term financial results. At all costs they have to increase their earnings every year. Just look at the display ads that *Fortune*, *The Wall Street Journal*, and similar publications regularly carry to extol companies' financial performance, with particular emphasis on their growth in per-share earnings. The most logical explanation for this is an attempt to drive up the price of their stock."

"Why do you think this is?" I asked. "Anyway, isn't management supposed to run the business in the interest of its stockholders?"

"I'll answer the first question first," replied MacCormick. "In many cases, I think top managers depend on stock prices of their companies to exercise stock options and to build up the value of their estates. I suppose tax laws have helped this trend along. Then, I think they feel that stock prices are measures of this operating success that are used not only by the Board of Directors within their own organization, but by others looking for candidates for top-level executive positions. So they base operating decisions heavily on their effect on short-term earnings, the very same criteria used most commonly by the financial community.

"As to what's wrong with running the business in the interest of the owners—that's another question. I don't want to get into that in detail now, but even if owners were the only group whose interest is involved, short-term earnings are of prime interest to speculators and institutional fund managers rather than long-term owners. I agree with Galbraith[10] that this distinction is important. If short-term results are emphasized to the detriment of the long-run competitive ability of the firm—which is one of the original issues we were discussing—surely the long-term owners' interest, the basis of capitalism as I see it, is being compromised in favor of the speculator and the manager of investment funds."

"Why does the subordinate manager, at whatever level, go along with this reduction of appraisal criteria to simple short-term financial measures? If I worked for a large firm I'd object. There's a lot more to a manager's job than that, and I can tell you that we wouldn't be in business long if I didn't think about the future," I commented self-righteously.

"Just as well you don't work for a lot of large firms I can think of," retorted MacCormick. "In spite of the underlying idea that the subordinate manager in an MBO system should substantially influence job objectives and the appraisal criteria to be used, because of pressures on the superior and the realities inherent in an organization hierarchy, that subordinate manager has little influence. Anyone who doesn't go along with the boss's view senses he or she will be replaced. I agree with you that in your relatively small business you wouldn't last long with this short-run view. But that's just it: I see this whole process catching on to become general and accepted practice in many American firms, particularly those of considerable size and with a variety of products and objectives. It's even being exported to Europe through seminars, and so on. Too bad for them!"

"But let's get back to the individual manager," I told him. "How does he or she react in terms of the operating decisions to be reached—after all, isn't that the stuff of the job?"

"Obviously, for any manager who goes along with the system, and as I said, really has no choice other than to leave the firm, survival and promotion are the name of the game, so these managers concern themselves with

the short-term results based on the indices involved—
usually the ratios I mentioned. They pay little attention
to the innovation and anticipation of future market
trends that are the basis for long-term growth and survival of the firm. It's ironic," he mused, "that society
grants the corporation everlasting life—unless it kills
itself—and yet in so many 'well-run' firms in this country, managers concentrate on the present and the past.

"Anyway, let's get back to the question of how all this
affects the individual manager's decision making. The
concentration on short-term performance leads him or
her to increase profitability *today*. This can be done by
cutting quality to the minimum level they can get away
with, either in terms of the quality control department
if they're at the production level, or their perception of
what the public will accept if they're at the policy-set-
ting level. They can also cut preventative maintenance,
although I suspect this is a less frequent practice. And
this in spite of the danger of decline in quality: I read
that Harvey Heinbach, the Merrill Lynch analyst, feels
that even given equal prices, U.S. car buyers prefer foreign cars, especially Japanese makes and VWs, because
of their superior quality."[11]

"I know," I interjected. "It's a hell of a job to incul-
cate pride of workmanship into a work force, particularly if the worker never had it or lost it somewhere
along the line. It's something you have to keep encour-
aging. You can't let down the standards to get the work
out on time. Boy, do you have to be careful of that,
because in the long run, you end up losing customers.
We'd be out of business in no time if we compromised
quality. Our customers impose tougher quality standards on vendors than they do on their own production
units, and we've learned this the hard way."

"Uh huh," MacCormick agreed somewhat impatiently. Obviously he didn't like being interrupted. "True enough, I suppose. You'd lose customers, as they will . . ." he muttered half to himself. "But that's not the worst part. The problem goes far beyond quality— that's relatively easy to cope with in the short run.

"I think the greater danger lies outside of quality or unit labor cost decisions. It's really in a set of attitudes that so easily pervade an organization, attitudes fostered by this preoccupation with short-term financial results and ratios. These include a new impetus to resist change on the production side. When I was an engineer in the works in Britain, we used to say to the plant people that if they had their way we'd still be producing the first model we ever made. Now we hear that making product changes loses the benefit of the 'learning curve,' as the current buzz word describes it, so dying products are still being produced long after their useful life in terms of satisfying *real* customer needs is over,[12] and that's just what foreign competition needs. Maybe the German and Japanese automobile manufacturers were lucky, in that most of their products have been fuel efficient for a long time in response to their governments' taxes on gasoline. Besides, foreign manufacturers have been exploiting the U.S. market for years. For many years our auto manufacturers never tried to combat this competition and have had to pay the price for their unwillingness to forego short-term profits in favor of preparing for production of vehicles that were clearly going to be customers' choices in view of the higher fuel costs ahead. Now they're finally getting the message, but not before their image and their beloved short-term profits have suffered grave damage.

"But this attitude goes beyond resistance to change and innovation," MacCormick continued. "If managers want to maximize their returns on the net assets assigned to them, besides doing all they can to increase the 'return figure,' they can improve their showing by lowering the denominator of the fraction in reducing the capital charged to them. They know this. Their notion of heaven is a fully depreciated plant that can barely maintain acceptable short-run unit costs. Given inflation at its present rate, they're very careful about adding new equipment—even when, as the economists would say, it makes good sense to substitute capital for labor. . . ."

"Yes, but hasn't current value accounting helped here?" I asked.

"I think it will eventually," MacCormick answered, "but I just hope it's soon. A lot of harm has been, and I'm afraid still is being done by resistance to and difficulties with CVA. This is one area where we neglected to see the impact of inflation on operating decisions in spite of early warnings by professional accountants. Some of these people even claim that many companies are still distributing assets as earnings because of their failure to allow adequately for inflation. This comes about because of their effort to maintain or even increase their payout every year so they can join what appears to me to be the growing list of firms whose institutional advertising claims the annual improvements in dividends and financial performance that I mentioned earlier."

"Are you suggesting that all this has affected the ability of the U.S. to compete internationally?" I asked.

"I sure am!" he replied with gusto. "I think that by and large, we're not as innovative as we once were. In addition, I'm convinced that in many industries we're undercapitalized in comparison with Japan, and we blame it all on government, or on an insufficient national savings rate which we say has limited capital formation, or on the unwillingness of Americans to work hard. All of these are factors to be sure. . . ."

"I can't go along with the lazy American workers argument," I broke in. "I've served my time in an assembly line, and in fact my son worked on one last summer. But the other two factors you mentioned certainly haven't helped much."

"Agreed," said MacCormick, "but my own opinion is that misapplied MBO, with its emphasis on short-run ratios, has been overlooked as an important reason why U.S. industry is undercapitalized in comparison with much of its foreign competition. For instance, I read somewhere that the Japanese auto worker makes about twice as many cars per year and almost twice as much steel as his American counterpart.[13] This kind of thing, coupled with the speed with which Japanese automate American plants like Motorola and invest large amounts of capital in new equipment in spite of the effect this must have on short-term operating results,[14] convinces me that it's not simply a matter of the Japanese or anyone else working harder than Americans. Neither is it simply attributable to government-business relations, nor a different attitude toward exports. While I think these are factors and important ones at that, the unidentified villain is, as I've just suggested, misapplied MBO. For this is the vehicle by which management attitudes toward innovation, both in product and in manufacturing, have been stifled. We may well be becoming what William Morris, founder, chairman, and CEO of Control Data Corporation calls a 'Risk-Avoiding Selfish Society' looking for immediate pay-offs,[15] failing to innovate to provide new jobs for the nation. Professional managers no longer take the long-term view as Alfred D. Chandler[16] says they do; in many large firms they are penalized if they do, and so instead they concentrate on the immediate short-term indices used to appraise them. Someone called this the MBA syndrome: a cautious no-risk management.[17] If this is characteristic of graduating MBAs—which may help to explain why the no-risk tendency seems to be so general—God knows big business is still on a hire-MBA kick." Here he paused and I jumped in.

"Small businesses like mine can't afford many MBAs, the one or two that we have are too busy to develop any kind of syndrome. If they did develop the no-risk tendency you spoke of, we couldn't keep them at my place. Risk is a way of life for us."

"I'd imagine it would be," MacCormick responded and thought for a moment. "I think there is one more problem as well, but you probably haven't encountered it directly—that's the disturbing tendency to cut back on R&D and, with a few exceptions, to emphasize applied research which promises a quicker and less uncertain payoff than basic research. Like everything else, R&D has become more expensive. In one sense it's a cost like any other one, and if it can be eliminated or minimized, so much the better for the payout-conscious manager's performance in the short run. After all, that's what counts in terms of personal advancement."

"How about government-underwritten research?" I asked. "Many firms like Textron, for example, pride themselves on the amount of research they do. In the case of Bell Helicopter, I'm sure some of it might be considered quite basic in its orientation."

"That's true I suppose," replied MacCormick, "and it's ironic that many firms that publicly decry the increasing influence of government on their operations claiming that it will put an end to free enterprise can also call on the government to supply funds or give tax breaks for increased research. You mentioned Textron and its research, much of which is government sponsored. Royal Little, its founder, once remarked that he saw his corporate executives as managers of capital rather than operators of businesses.[18] It seems to me that many U.S. firms have lost much of their customer orientation, the focus on customers' needs which was so strongly advocated by Theodore Levitt in 'Marketing Myopia.'[19] There is a disturbing tendency instead to let others go first, and if they're successful, jump in too or, even better, buy them out! Because of short-term cost considerations and perhaps the 'not-invented-here syndrome,' innovation often comes from outside the industry. It's Texas Instruments and firms like it who have really been heavily responsible for revolutions in calculating machines and even in the watch industry. Sure the long-established firms followed, but they've had to play catch-up ball and some may never recapture the industry domination they once exercised."

"Can you think of any firms that are relatively less affected by this preoccupation with short-term profits to the detriment of long-term growth and survival?" I asked. Sure I'm concerned with making money each quarter, I thought to myself, but our few shareholders are in for the long pull, and thank God for that.

"I'm glad you asked. As a matter of fact I've been thinking about this question quite a bit lately. At least three groups stand out in my mind, although again they overlap to a considerable degree. First, there are those companies that have made a strong effort to resist this tendency and to think constantly about the future. Their organizations are prepared for it because they've adopted policies to encourage innovation and back them up with the funds needed for R&D and investment in plant and equipment, even to the detriment of short-run profitability: IBM, 3M, Xerox, and of course TI, which we've already mentioned, may well fall into this group. Second, firms where ownership is heavily represented in management, and this is the expressed desire of the owners—sometimes because of what is all-too-often disparagingly referred to as social conscience, sometimes I suppose because of a desire that the product bearing the owner's name be recognized as reflecting higher quality and the state of the art; maybe Johnson & Johnson and Michelin belong here. Third, firms in a near-monopoly position in their industry or segment of an industry; Eastman Kodak, AT&T, and IBM again might be examples. Does the list sound familiar? Enlightened firms maybe?"

"Where is this preoccupation with short-term performance, misapplied MBO, or whatever you call it going to take us?" I asked, thinking I might as well hear out this prophet of doom.

"Well we've mentioned some of the trends: declining R&D expenditures with the slower pace of innovation that results, declining productivity of labor, and minimal quality levels will, if unchecked, all lead to increased competition from abroad on the home market and a rough road for American products overseas. But there are other less obvious implications of the short-run profit orientation of misapplied MBO; for example, businesses have placed a new emphasis on marketing in the narrowest sense of the word—new packaging and new sales campaigns rather than products designed to fit changing customer needs. You see, this approach is less costly, and it has led to a large number of ill-suited, expensive, and heavily advertised products being foisted on an increasingly dissatisfied group of American consumers who are not only resisting their purchase and turning abroad to what they see as better value, but also seeing militant consumerism as their only realistic recourse. . . ."

"Wait a minute," I interrupted. "I remember being told in a marketing course that mass marketing and

mass production depend on each other. You really can't
have one without the other. Aren't you simply taking
the old, somewhat tired engineering view that marketing is 'soft,' not hard like product design or production,
and therefore is a frill of less intrinsic merit?"

"I certainly am not," he replied with some irritation.
"Surely you can't believe I'm *that* stupid. Clearly marketing is essential. I remember a few things from my
marketing courses, too, mainly that building a better
mousetrap isn't enough for business success: people
have to know about it or else they can't buy it. I'm not
the least ashamed of being an engineer—have you ever
met an engineer who was? But that's just it: the point is
that the product should really *be* better. I'm sick of mar-
keters' phony, catchy claims of better performance than
the competition's virtually identical offering. Through
increased product cost, the public has to pay dearly for
having been deceived, and that's nuts. Look at this—"
MacCormick reached for a paperback he had in his
pocket. "This is what I mean. See what the writer says
about his own experience?" He read from the book.
" 'There was this product called Plunge. All I had to do
was read three words. Plunge works fast. In spite of my
off-hand delivery, they used my three words in over a
hundred commercials. The money from this put one of
my children through two years of college.'[20] That's bad
enough, but when you add the cost of TV production
and time charges—WOW! God, that sort of thing makes
me sick—the product was probably good old caustic
soda anyway. Marketing innovation is replacing product innovation because it's less risky in terms of its effect on the principal criteria used under misapplied
MBO (ROI or contribution to earnings). It takes less
money to repackage or reintroduce an old product than
to produce a new one. If it works, fine; if not, then you
look for another way to go with an improved campaign

based on marketing research. Form is less expensive to modify than substance, I guess. But I find little value in creating a 'need' in the mind of a gullible consumer by razzle-dazzle manipulative advertising and then satisfying it at ridiculous cost to consumers who can ill afford this victimization. I suppose I'm just a simple engineer at heart, as you mentioned earlier."

"But what are the consequences of all this?" I asked. For a simple engineer you certainly are articulate, I added to myself.

"Hard to know where to begin, but we've already identified some of the more obvious ones. Consumers, clearly, are being offered less satisfactory products for more money and are turning to foreign producers for satisfaction while complaining loudly and demanding more government regulation of business. And U.S. producers are feeling the impact of consumer disenchantment: all U.S. automobile manufacturers reported losses in 1980. Even GM cut its dividend in 1980, and it's interesting, too, that its German operations have been more seriously affected by the sales slump that has hit the auto industry than have domestic producers in that country.[21] The auto industry uses more steel, glass, and rubber than any other, so a decline in that sector affects many other industries. Consumer electronics companies have been battered by Japanese competition, as has steel. You can go on and on. Then clearly, layoffs have affected employment levels, and new jobs are not being created fast enough. But it goes even further than that. The growth rate of American productivity has slowed, and though I don't place too much stock in figures of this kind, according to a New York Stock Exchange study,[22] the U.S. ranked sixth in economic performance among the eight major industrial nations between 1974 and 1980. But what particularly disturbs me is what it's doing to our self-image and our image abroad as the world leader and chief exponent of free enterprise. For many people, both at home and abroad, the American dream, based on our ability to achieve what we seek, seems to be fading. We seem to be lagging rather than leading and have seemingly lost the managerial leadership we once had for other countries who followed our earlier examples."

"OK, you've listed enough problems to overwhelm me. I know consultants specialize in the identification of problems, but as a businessman I'm far more interested in finding solutions. How do we get out of this trap?" I asked.

This guy is too glib, I thought to myself, and he's making me defensive as hell. After all, we've done damn well as a nation, and I guess I see our present situation as a pause in our progress rather than a turning point—a pause brought about by the combination of a normal cyclical downturn and the oil crisis. I'm getting a bit tired of listening to Britons telling us about the folly of America and Americans. OK, MacCormick, put up or shut up.

"Glad you asked," he replied. "The problem is difficult and multifaceted, and so is the solution. I agree with Peter Drucker that the first step in dealing with any situation of this complexity is problem definition.[23] In this instance I believe we can say that, with exceptions, U.S. industry is in danger of losing the dynamism it once had, that American consumers are being wooed away by foreign competitors who offer what they believe to be more suitable, better products at a lower price, and that stockholders are going to pay in the long run, as for that matter are workers and the economy as a whole. . . ."

"How can you separate industry, consumers, and workers from each other?" I interrupted. "They're overlapping categories."

"Touché, they are indeed," he acknowledged. "The point is, if America continues along its present path, we're all going to suffer. Let's look then for what Drucker calls the critical factor, that which must be changed before anything else can be changed, moved, or acted upon.[24] I'm concerned that the critical factor here is that U.S. managers are increasingly taking the short-term rather than long-term view in strategic decision making, and that short-run profitability has become more important to them than long-term growth or survival. As I said earlier, professional managers, according to Chandler, are supposed to behave in exactly the opposite fashion, but I don't think most of them do anymore—at least not in my experience. Even acquisitions are often being made on the basis of their effect on this year's earnings, not on the basis of the synergistic effect or on the likelihood that they'll increase the competitive ability of the firm. Per share earnings or ROI are what affect stock prices, and that's what counts. God knows the market is more responsive to short-term operating results than long-run prospects. This emphasis on the short run then permeates the entire hierarchy. You see, misapplied MBO is reflected in managerial decision making at all levels. For me, the way out begins with a new emphasis on the long term at all levels of management, and a corresponding deemphasis on blaming government, particularly at the federal level, for all the troubles and difficulties encountered by American business and its managers."

"But surely you would admit that the government could do even more to stimulate the economy and encourage innovation through tax credits and so forth," I asked a bit testily. "Besides, you have no idea of the extent to which small businesses like ours are harrassed by government regulations covering about every aspect of our operations and subjected to incredible and unnecessary expense because of the additional staff required to submit countless reports, many of which ask for essentially the same information in slightly different forms. I'm convinced it's harder on us than it is on the giant corporations."

"OK, OK," he answered. "I'm not saying they couldn't do a hell of a lot more at all levels. I am saying that complaining that the government is the largest cause of the decline in the ability of U.S. firms to compete more effectively, both domestically and abroad, will not solve the problem. You can't call them in to help ailing businesses with massive loans from taxpayers' pockets, expect heavy support for R&D programs, and so forth, and at the same time, expect them to leave you alone to run your own business. That just doesn't make sense. Sure they could do a lot more, but they'll never do as much as business wants.

"But let's get back to the problem of what U.S. firms can do themselves to improve their own innovative and productive capabilities. Productivity and innovation are the keys to improved competitive ability, and they both involve vision and risk of failure. Misapplied MBO discourages both of these as far as managers are concerned. Fear of failure and overemphasis on short-run performance makes risk and innovation unwise actions for the manager. Organizations must see to it that innovative objectives, in terms of both product and process, are included in the establishment of performance targets for each manager and rewards for success provided. At the same time the risks associated with occasional failures must be mitigated in the same way.

"Owners of small businesses live with the risk of failure most days of their lives," he went on, "and they have learned to cope with it. They take chances because they have to if they're to compete against large firms in the business of satisfying customers. You know that better than I do. But as a result they're innovative in many instances, and their innovations can upset old industries and create new ones, as we've already discussed. MBO must be seen by managers in large firms as rewarding risk taking and occasionally tolerating the failures or disappointments that are bound to arise from time to time. That's what's supposed to happen and so rarely does in the large firms I'm familiar with."

"I know I'm hopping back to an old point," I interrupted. "But how about some further government concessions for small companies, beyond SBA loans which are hard to get, slow, and all too often most available to the companies that don't need them."

"I might go for that," he said. "But you know more about that than I do. Most of my clients are larger or middle-sized firms, and my concern is naturally concentrated there. Somehow, they have to realize that *real* innovation is the way you win customers, as this is the basis for real price and product competition. This innovation has got to start coming from within, and not in response to government pressures, as was the case with seat belts and high-impact bumpers, or as a belated reaction to foreign competition. Mature organizations fight change in so many instances and so seldom reward it. Maybe the use of a committee of seasoned businesspeople with an occasional consultant," he added with a smile, "might help to appraise new ideas more objectively and get away from this tendency to start with the old and shun the new or the 'not-invented-here.' Some firms are doing this now."

At that point the loudspeaker called our flight, and MacCormick got up and started to arrange his books and carryon luggage. "I enjoyed our chat," I said, shaking hands with him.

"So did I," he replied. "Good luck at the trade show."

I walked toward the gate thinking to myself how I'd like to find U.S. equipment I could bring to our firm with a clear conscience. Maybe if what MacCormick said were heard in the right quarters, the U.S. could win back a lot of the business it's lost. I still believe in Yankee ingenuity. . . .

MacIntosh

THE NEW YORK–LONDON flight was already forty-five minutes late as I took my seat in first class. I wonder how much longer I can justify this luxury, I thought, but it's more comfortable when you're well over six feet tall, and occasionally you do run into some interesting high-level people—even the odd foreign dignitary with his retinue nowadays. Damn it all, I work hard! Only presidents of small manufacturing companies know the pressure we're under to keep enough business in the shop at the right price without going overboard, and the IRS makes perks an important part of the compensation package. Settling into an aisle seat halfway down the port side of the aircraft, I noticed that MacCormick, the consultant I talked with in the lounge during the flight delay, was in an aisle seat on the other side of the plane. He exchanged a few words with his neighbor, then leaned back in a resting position. No wonder, I thought; he must have been talked out!

After a couple of minutes a young chap in his mid-thirties, of medium height and a good build, which showed off his superbly tailored suit, sat down in the seat next to me. He reached over and shook hands just after we became airborne.

"MacIntosh here," he said with a slight Canadian roll of his *r*. "On my way to London, then Scotland, looking for cloth for my clothing business—we still get a lot of our good stuff there. What's your line?" he asked with a smile.

"I run a small metal parts manufacturing operation outside of Toledo. I'm on a buying trip, too, only I'm looking at machine tools," I told him.

"I was sitting near you in the waiting room, behind you, actually, so you probably didn't notice. I couldn't help overhearing your conversation with that sleepy consultant over there," he explained, motioning toward the dozing MacCormick in the front of the cabin. "Boy, he sure could talk, that one. No question about it, he really made some good points, but I've sort of had a bellyful of consultants lately."

"How so?" I asked, even though I was afraid that I was opening another bottle of conversational champagne and that I wouldn't be able to get the cork back in until it had run dry. Anyway, they say you tend to learn while listening rather than talking, and the young man next to me at least looked impressive.

"Well, my Dad started his own clothing business in Toronto after moving the family from Nova Scotia, where I was born. I guess his timing, luck, and pretty good business sense resulted in a fair measure of success. He got a few government contracts, and since he'd learned the value of good quality and service from his father, who was a tailor in the old country, these were his watchwords. Anyway, the business grew, and he had a good-size operation going when he retired two years ago and handed over the reins to me."

"Is he still active in the company?" I asked.

"Not really. Oh, he's still chairman of the board, but as long as we pay a good dividend, he's content to busy himself with hybrid roses, particularly the new species he's trying to develop, called the 'White MacIntosh.' He feels he's worked hard enough, and so do I. Anyway, we're trying to expand, because in our business it's grow or die. That's why I've been in New York, to add some U.S. outlets. But getting back to the subject of consultants, I've had occasion to use them several times recently, and I won't say they haven't been useful, because they have. But frankly, they haven't done as well as I thought they would; I guess I've been, well, disappointed."

"Before you start telling me the reasons, let me ask you one question. Why did you feel you needed outside help anyway? I'm sure you were raised to believe in the innate virtues of decisive, self-reliant decision making?"

"After Dad retired from an active role in the business and left me in charge," MacIntosh replied, "I decided I needed to take a really cold look at our operation, where it was at the time, where it was likely to be in the future, and what we should be doing now. You know, strategic planning kinds of things. My problem was that I'd always been so close to the business and its problems. As far back as I can remember, Dad was talking about it to Mother and to his friends who'd visit us at home. Then I had summer jobs in the shop and finally got even more familiar with it when I filled in for office people taking their summer holidays. In a word, I was just steeped in the business; so steeped I really couldn't see it objectively and I needed to talk with someone who could look at it from an informed, detached, professional perspective. I needed someone who could take a nonpartisan view, if you like, and could indeed see the forest for the trees."

"So you figured a consultant could do this better than anyone else?" I asked.

"Uh huh, friends whose opinions I respected certainly wouldn't have the time for anything like this, and then I'm not at all sure most of them wouldn't soft-pedal the bad news aspects of their conclusions. I guess I felt I needed expert help on a short-term basis to do a job I had neither the time nor the objectivity to do myself."

"How well did your consultant do at getting a feel for your operation?" I asked.

"She was good, and fast too, at this phase. She knew how to ask cutting, pertinent questions. It was easy to see she'd developed her skills along this line with previous clients. Besides her professional status, she had the ability to gain the trust and confidence of my subordinates, and this resulted in her getting more open, honest answers from some of them than I could have, even if I'd asked exactly the same questions. I've heard the old saying that consultants borrow your watch to answer your query as to what time it is, but if they're capable, they do better at getting at the heart of the matter than you could do yourself. I suppose it's hard to be totally honest with your boss." MacIntosh paused reflectively. "I hadn't really thought much about this, but I guess many of my people saw the consultant as a concrete and costly indication of my determination to make some changes if they seemed appropriate, and that *I* wanted them to open up and express their opinions as to what changes were needed. Dad was a bit dictatorial, kind of a self-made man who had a lot of confidence in his ability to make the best decisions himself. 'Pooled ignorance never results in knowledge,' he used to say. Anyway, while the consultant was going about her work I could sense that most of my people felt good about her being there. There were some of course, a few of whom are full-time sourpusses, who thought it was a waste of money that could have been better directed toward improving their own paychecks. As for me, I confess that I had a feeling of mild euphoria too," he added with a self-conscious smile.

"Why was that?" I asked.

"Well, I guess primarily because I felt that at last someone was working on a problem I'd been aware of for quite a while, a problem that as I mentioned a minute ago, I kept telling myself rightly or wrongly I didn't have the time, inclination, or maybe even the expertise to deal with. Someone with specialized training and experience was dealing with the situation, and the gun was at her head. What more could I do about it than give it to an expert? I slept better knowing that even if she didn't come up with anything new, then that meant we weren't doing so badly and if she did, well we could weigh its merits, then decide. At last I had someone I could talk to about my innermost business fears, someone who would listen and evaluate carefully, a sort of confessor-figure who could give encouragement or advice. As you know, it's sometimes lonely at the top."

"That's for sure," I replied. "And I think I read you. In a sense you were enjoying what T. S. Eliot calls the 'luxury of an intimate disclosure to a stranger.'"[1] I was pleased with my literary allusion. "It was someone whose criticism you could accept or reject and act accordingly, whose sympathetic presence gave you an opportunity to get your worries off your chest."

"I suppose so, but I certainly hadn't thought of it in *that* way. As I said, I felt better about things while she was on the job. That's as far as I want to go."

"Not quite far enough for me," I countered. I had a couple of comments of my own to make about the psychological benefits of consultants. "I suspect you probably also enjoyed the feeling of prestige that your use of a consultant gave you among your business associates. You could say to your buddies, 'I have Jones, you know, of Smith, Jones, and Brown, working on some of our strategic problems.' It shows you're a serious and responsible business executive. Besides, in your case it might even impress the members of the board of directors, if they didn't make the recommendation to use an outsider in the first place," I added with a smile to ease what might have been considered a nasty comment.

"I guess so; that's probably partly true, but only to a very limited extent," he admitted grudgingly.

"I don't see anything wrong with that. No need to feel guilty; as you say, it's lonely in the CEO spot. But you said at the beginning of our discussion that you'd had a bellyful of consultants lately, and yet, up to now, your account of your recent experience with them seems by and large to have been pretty favorable. Your woman was objective and professional in her approach. She was skilled in getting information from your people, in some cases better than you could have elicited yourself. She dealt with problems you didn't want to tackle for one reason or another, problems you now felt were being handled by an expert who was going to have to produce an objective report and evaluation of the total situation in a reasonable time. And so you felt better, slept better, and had something to brag about to your pals and even your board. So what are your complaints?" I asked.

"OK, I was just getting to those. You may remember it was you who asked how I came to use consultants in the first place," he chided. "But before I get down to criticisms, I want to mention one more type of situation where I've used a consultant. I've also had to use outsiders to help me with the design and installation of new systems and for the solution of technical problems that came about because of changing technology. To put it simply, we occasionally require expert help on a one-shot basis. For example, we recently opted for a computer-based management information system, and we needed help with the technical and staffing changes required to make it effective. Then too, we ran into technical difficulties when we considered and later installed laser machines in the cloth-cutting department. We needed solutions, but we couldn't afford to add additional permanent staff to get them.

"Anyway, back to complaints," he continued. "I don't know quite how to put my major one, except to say that often when I'm using consultants I have the sneaking suspicion that their prime concerns revolve around acquiring a client. This they do by pointing out how urgently the organization requires their services and how much better the operation should and can subsequently be. Then, once they've completed this selling activity, they try to do everything possible to find a need for additional assignments which they can perform themselves or for which they can supply additional experts with the proper qualifications."

"I guess they're in business like anyone else—a client is a source of income. Just as Drucker says, they're in the business of creating (and satisfying, I might add) customers.[2] Like you, they have to make selling trips, many of which don't pan out, and if they're going to pay expenses and make a profit, they have to follow up to retain contracts. Let's be fair about this."

"No one's objecting to that," he said a bit testily. "But just like lawyers and doctors, they're supposed to be professionals. Yet I often have the feeling their recommendations as to what needs doing are heavily affected by self-interest, while I'm the one who's footing the bill. . . ."

"Oh, come on, let's not get off on that lawyer-doctor kick! It would seem to me that every profession has its share of opportunists," I interrupted. "Let's get back to specific criticisms."

"OK, OK, I was getting carried away, I guess. I'll be more precise. Let's just say I feel they tend to overstate the need for their services. Surely you won't object to that." Hearing no protests, MacIntosh continued, "Another feeling I have along this line actually runs in the opposite direction. It's that in some cases they may try to tell me what they think I want to hear. I get the feeling that they try to sense out what my position is on a particular problem they've been asked to explore. Then they cast their recommendations in these lines, almost currying favor and afraid to offend, lest I shoot the messenger who brings me the bad news."

I glanced at the front of the cabin, wondering whether MacCormick could hear this discussion. Just as I looked up he changed his position and tipped his reclining seat even further back. He'd obviously opted for sleep.

"Well at least there seemed to be somewhat countervailing forces operating on the consultant: find new problems whether or not they need attention, and yet be sensitive to the fact that the client is usually to a considerable extent responsible for their existence. I suppose you do have to rely on the professionalism of the consultant, whatever that is, to get an accurate perspective, but that's life. You always have to evaluate sources of information for yourself; that's part of being an executive," I mused. "Continue."

"All right. I think another complaint I have is that they tend to seek similarities between my organizational situation and that of other firms that they've had as clients. I'm not sure how well I'm putting this, and I'm aware that in looking for a consultant a prime consideration is the reputation of the clientele and previous assignments, but I have the distinct impression that consultants tend to try to apply solutions to our situation that they have worked out for other clients and that they often force-fit them into our situation, even if they have to bend our case to fit their solutions."

"I think I follow you, but can you be more specific?"

"I'll try: usually, if not almost always, consultants we call in to help us with problems have dealt with similar cases before or they've developed an approach to get at their solutions; heaven knows there's nothing wrong there. But the difficulty comes when they also develop a limited number of solutions and are convinced that these solutions are optimal for all organizations. It's almost as if they start with a few preconceived solutions and then try to find evidences of the set of problems to which they can be applied. I'm not saying it's always deliberate, but I think there is this tendency to suggest solutions already worked out for other consulting assignments. For example, it might be as simple as applying a solution developed rather specifically for a large organization to a much smaller one, or vice versa."

"Again, can you be more specific? What's the problem here?"

"Just that the solution offered can be clinically optimal and yet fail totally because the organization rejects it for one or both of two related reasons. First, the managers responsible for implementation may sabotage it because it runs against their image of themselves and their roles in the organization. They may feel, for instance, that it will affect their status because they didn't think of it themselves or that it may disrupt the hierarchy and diminish their influence. Or they may feel it violates their concept of what the organization has always stood for and that any change in this will spell doom. Second, the consultant may have been either insensitive to, or even worse, unaware of the importance and the impact of the hierarchy and organizational culture on the daily lives of the members of the organization. This sort of thing occurred at our place not long ago when we had a young hot-shot consultant with a brand-new graduate degree come in to help us with the new management information system that I mentioned earlier. His prime interest was in the elegance and sophistication of its design, and he ran roughshod over the sensitivities of the people who would have to implement it."

"Maybe they were only tender because they hadn't been smart or sophisticated enough themselves to come up with a workable plan on their own and would have fought any changes, sort of a combination of the not-invented-here syndrome with an inherent resistance to any change," I put in, astutely.

"Uh huh," MacIntosh acknowledged. "Maybe, but his insensitivity to people and his lack of organizational sophistication slowed the implementation of our new system to a crawl. We finally had to ask the outfit we had retained to send us someone else, and they did."

"What was the second consultant like?" I asked. Sooner or later we were going to have to do something about our MIS—or more accurately, our lack of one. I might as well learn from someone else's mistakes.

"Technically less at the threshold, but infinitely better at getting the cooperation and support of our people. Funny, but technical expertise so often brings with it insensitivity to the world of others," he observed. "Anyway we finally did get the job done, but it took longer than it should have, and we lost one of our better people who got fed up and quit. I suppose he might have been ready to leave anyway, and he did get a good job. . . ."

"Would you use the same consultants again?" I asked.

"I think so. They did develop a good system, and in the end they stuck with it until it was operating properly. The first fellow couldn't deal with the human problems he caused, but after I leaned on the principal in charge of his office, they finally dealt with those too. No, in fairness, I can't say they walked away. They felt responsible for the whole job, unlike some outfits in the consulting game that I've heard about."

"I sometimes use a business school professor as a consultant," I put in.

"I've thought of that, but never really tried it. A few of my friends have, though. One of my tennis pals, who's a consultant himself, calls them his 'low overhead competitors' and makes disapproving comments about the applicability of 'ivory tower' solutions to real business problems."

"No question that they do have lower overhead," I replied. "Many of them don't maintain offices. Their regular employers pay for their insurance, pension, and so on. Besides, they often have access to computer facilities at minimum cost and use students to whom they either pay a pittance or grant academic credit for the tedious time-consuming legwork. Anyway they're less expensive, and for a small operation like mine that's an important consideration. You get a lot of expertise for the money."

"OK," replied MacIntosh. "But how about the applicability of their ethereal solutions to concrete managerial problems?"

"Obviously, I'm in no position to generalize. I haven't really used the full-time variety to any extent. But my guess is that you run into many of the same problems you mentioned, some to a lesser extent and some greater," I replied.

"Now it's my turn to ask *you* to be specific," said MacIntosh with a somewhat self-satisfied smile.

"I'll try. Some professors went into academia after quite a few years of real-world experience, but you can find full-time consultants who did the same thing and are also worldly wise. Many have regular contact with businesspeople through lecturing, management development, and consultant activities, but probably most don't have as much current real-world involvement as their full-time counterparts—slight edge to the full timers. Most profs have more formal education and more skill in persuasion—slight edge to the profs. I could go on and on. . . ."

"Don't. At least not in that way," said MacIntosh irritably. "I'm looking for information this time around. Let me pick your brain, *specifically* please. Which of the problems I mentioned encountering with full timers did you run into with the low overhead folks, and were there any additional ones? Damn it all, I'm going to nail you down!"

I sounded a bit like a professor myself. "OK, but realize I'm talking exclusively from my own experience." Sure I was hedging, but how can you generalize about the professor-consultant? God knows how varied they are.

"My suspicion is that perhaps they're less single-minded in their determination to retain clients. Sure, they probably need and seek money as much, if not more than their full-time competition; but they do know that whether they're retained or not they're sure of their regular stipends. So they're a bit less under the gun to cultivate business.

"I have the sense too that the profs I've used have been overly brutal, rather than overly sensitive in their reports to me and my subordinates and have rather en-

joyed telling me what I obviously would not like to
hear. I should be able to deal with that, but sometimes
my subordinates aren't. Maybe it's because they spend
so much time dealing with students and administrators
from a personal power base that profs lose sight of the
role that sheer power plays in an organization and its
effect on the psychological well-being of its members."

"OK. That's better. I think I understand you. You're
saying that they've lost sight of the impact of power
relationships and their effect on people because the
world in which they normally act is a world of conversation, computers, coffee, and collegiality," MacIntosh
replied, not displeased with his own rhetoric. "Along
the same line, I wouldn't expect them to be as sophisticated as the full-time consultant about interdivisional
relationships and rivalries and the extent to which corporate welfare often plays second fiddle to divisional
performance. When it comes to a choice between the
two, the divisional managers, in spite of textbooks, usually decide in favor of their own team; at least that's the
way it was when I worked briefly for a big corporation
right after graduation. I'd guess they might be a bit less
aware of the political games that go on, the use of the
coverup, cult of the personality, and so on. Is this accurate?"

"I think that's probably right," I allowed. "Then
there's another feeling I have, and that is that the professor is looking at me and at my organization with an
eye to collecting case and lecture material. I feel as
though we're all on a dissecting table and that the
results of the examination, admittedly in disguised
form because of their obsession with professional privi-
lege, may find its way into case books, journals, and
classrooms. I confess it makes me a bit uncomfortable,
and I have to overcome a desire to withhold informa-

tion that might be frowned upon or criticized. It may be because I still see him as a professor—perhaps role ambiguity is at the root of it. That's what our man would say. He loves big words.

"Then there's the related feeling that, once they diagnose our problem, they'll use us as a lab to try out original solutions and see how they work in a real-world situation, and then use the findings in a research report. Profs are often a faddish lot too. . . ."

"How do you mean?" pursued MacIntosh.

"Well, one day they're all on fire about PERT. The next, it's job enrichment, or cognitive dissonance, or distributed data processing, or transactional analysis, then cybernetics, and so on. I sometimes feel that they deliberately see everything in these terms. Force-fitting preconceived solutions as you called it, but solutions they've read about somewhere or worked out in a lab rather than solutions from previous consulting assignments, although I'm sure they do that too."

"Anything else?" MacIntosh asked.

"Just one point," I replied. "I think business school professors have become overly specialized, and when they go into consulting they often see problems too narrowly from the point of view of their own particular field of interest. It's natural enough, I suppose."

"Can you give me an example?" he asked.

"Marketing profs often see an organization's primary problems almost entirely in marketing terms. They want all kinds of marketing research, consumer behavior studies, and so on, as a basis for any organizational actions. Accountants feel that a good MIS system in place will solve all difficulties and so on. Even the generalists, the business policy people, have problems. In their devotion to a long-term perspective and setting up organizations to deal with the needs of tomorrow's customers, uncertain at best, they tend to forget we have to satisfy today's customers and today's standards if we're still going to be in business and able to compete effectively at some future time.

"It took us a while to find a good one, but I think we have one now. We have to keep an eye on him though," I added. Just then, fortunately, the flight attendant arrived and asked us for our drink orders. "I'll have a double bourbon and soda," I said.

Not unexpectedly MacIntosh ordered Scotch. Neat with no ice.

"Well," he said. "Let's at least have a drink to 'em. They're a pain in the ass, and you sure gotta watch 'em. But they're useful, I suppose. . . ."

reputations. It's the only way they survive and grow, so they certainly don't oversell or underdeliver." MacCormick was getting a bit steamed up. As for me, I was not that emotionally involved with the issue, and I admit I was enjoying watching his somewhat defensive attitude take form.

"How about professors as consultants? Anything you want to add or did we cover it all?" I asked.

"Not a lot really. As I told you, I've been both, and I think you covered it pretty well. There are good and bad ones on both sides of the fence. No question that you get more credentials for less money with academics, and after all, most of our people started under their tutelage. Both varieties have access to specialists in particular consulting areas. We would agree that, as a group, we have more practical experience and maybe more skill in implementation, which they would counter by claiming that they're better at conceptualization and more objective. Naturally I'm biased in favor of experience with a greater variety of clients; otherwise I'd still be an academic arguing for the superiority of my team. As a group we're more realistic," he added somewhat pompously and went on.

"But that's not what I wanted to talk about; I have to set a few things straight. That relocated Blue Nose, MacIntosh, indicated that his experience with consultants had not been quite up to what he'd hoped. He was kind of dumping on the profession, but we've become used to being the butt of business jokes. Even if most of their punch lines haven't got much punch. Would you like to hear the other side of the story?"

He didn't give me time to answer, but just purred on in that smooth, convincing manner of his. Not that it really mattered to me. He was interesting, and "turnabout is fair play."

"Let's begin at the beginning. When an executive decides to bring in a consultant, or perhaps it's the boss who decides to get someone outside the organization to look the situation over, they're often a bit uneasy about the whole business."

"Why is this?" I asked. "I don't feel that way at all." Now *I* was getting on the defensive. Better watch it, Riter!

"Well, I think in some cases they wonder whether they shouldn't be able to do the whole job themselves and feel that they're shirking a responsibility that's really part of their assignment," replied MacCormick. "This is less likely the case when the consulting assignment is of a narrower, highly technical nature, I might add. Then there's the matter of fees, which I think is troublesome to managers on two counts: first they can't resist comparing the daily rate being charged with their own salaries, and it seems too high. We *really* don't make all that much you know. . . ."

My mind drifted. He looks well-heeled to me: those shoes are hand-made; the immaculately pressed and tailored blue blazer didn't come off the rack, and that striped silk tie looks like the one I passed up as too expensive in the men's boutique at Marshall Fields in Chicago last month. He's retired, and still he travels first class; bet he has a Cadillac. No—more likely a Mercedes or a BMW. "Oh, come on, MacCormick, don't give me that stuff," I thought to myself, but he was still flowing on.

"Second, they wonder whether the counsel they receive will be worth more to them personally than the additional cost they have to absorb, along with its effect on their earnings. In a word, they're not sure whether the consultant is an avoidable expense and feel a little guilty. Of course, this would be easier to take if they had been told to use an 'expert,' but then they'd be less concerned about the success or failure of the project. This attitude makes things more difficult for the consultant, and so it goes. It's hard for a consultant to transcend these external, inhibiting factors and get down to dealing with the real issues. All this leads to my second set of complaints about businesspeople and things that waste my time, and incidentally, their money." He paused to see whether he had my full attention.

This time he did. Maybe we're getting down to where the "rubber meets the road," I thought. I have to admit to being a bit defensive when I hear gratuitous criticisms about our clan from the outside, particularly from hot shots who've never met a payroll or have forgotten all the pressure and tension that's involved in keeping a business going, let alone growing. I looked (or was it glared?) at his gray eyes and said, "Fire away, let's get down to those complaints."

"OK, back to the beginning, at the stage where someone high up in the organization decides that it might be a good idea to use an outside person to take a look at some aspect of the operation, and a decision is made to hire a consultant. No, on second thought, let's go back even farther than that, because my first complaint enters the picture earlier."

"You've lost me." What the hell is he talking about, I asked myself.

"Keep your shirt on, I'm trying to think out loud. *This* consultant, at least, hasn't got neatly tabulated solutions to everything that comes up, which might incidentally come up as a surprise to that Canuck you were sitting with." MacCormick sniffed a bit more audibly than was absolutely essential to clear his nasal passages. "What I mean is that, for misguided reasons of economy or feelings that 'we should be able to handle this perfectly well in-house,' we're called in to deal with a situation that has become—how can I put it?—inflamed by inadequate and often downright unfit actions on the part of the organization's staff. Our first task then is to calm things down, which takes time and costs the client money."

"Can you give me a for instance?" I asked.

"Certainly. My only problem is to pick one from so many. OK, suppose you're thinking of installing an MIS. No doubt you're going to have to do something about this one of these days." MacCormick gave me a superior look. "You call in a representative of all the hardware suppliers you've heard of: IBM, Digital, Honeywell, maybe Wang too. You become confused, realize you're going to have to add someone to your staff who not only knows what these people are talking about and can dish it back, but who can also cut through their BS which is designed to sell you as much as they can get away with. Suppose you choose the right person (there'll be some measure of luck involved if you do, because chances are you'll either hire and have to pay for more expertise than you need, or you'll hire less and pay for it in a different way), but let's say you do get a good person and she starts choosing equipment. Unless she's unusual she runs into problems because of her biases in favor of the equipment on which she has been trained; this is a minor problem, however, compared to a natural desire on her part to empire-build with all kinds of unneeded capacity available to expand the operation. Demand for computer services expands mysteriously to absorb supply, often with diminishing marginal utility, but that's another story. Suffice it to say that she may well not choose what's needed in terms of its ability to meet the needs of your organization for a *reasonable* length of time. She may not make the best decision as to how much should be leased or bought, nor how much and what kind of stuff *you*, not *she*, *really* needs. Remember, all this is costing money in the long run, too, because future commitments are involved. There are so many chances to make expensive mistakes even up to this point, but hers are just beginning. . . ."

"What do you mean—beginning?" I asked, a bit dismayed, to put it mildly.

"Next you face the problem of systems design to meet the needs of the organization as an organization *and*, what's most important, the needs of the managers as people—a delicate balance. It's a matter of neither under- nor overselling *and* of careful reassurance. Human beings are not predictable like machines. More mistakes are made; things start going wrong. People become miffed, start fighting, and then we're called in. At this point, the situation has gotten out of hand, and we have to try to make the best of it with hardware and personnel we probably wouldn't have chosen in the first place. Managers are at war with each other, and a poorly designed system has to be rebuilt almost from the ground up. We're called in to try and patch up something that could have been set up properly and much less expensively from the beginning. We know what we're doing, not just because we're smart (which we are), but also because we've done it before.

"Same is true in terms of other forms of consulting: ill-fated management development programs that are set up around human relations concepts because 'these never hurt anyone and they may even do some good.' They don't work, and then either the program is scuttled after a great waste of time and money or we're called in." MacCormick was talking fast now.

"Now it's your turn to slow down," I told him. "Why human relations?"

"OK, maybe I went too far that time," MacCormick

allowed. "It could have just as easily been job enrichment, interpersonal skills, and so on. The point is that the development program is centered on what the training person, or more likely the unfortunate who has been given this additional duty, feels can be done with minimal strain and least chance of total failure. After it's flopped, we get called in, go about it professionally, analyze training needs, make recommendations, and put on a program, but we face the handicap of having to live down the bad odor left by the previous failure. Same problem—called in too late, and our job is a lot more difficult and costly than it would have been if we'd been called in before people started spending money."

"OK, consultants often get called in too late. Anything else at the early stages?" I probed. Here was a chance to get free curbstone consulting advice—or was it partly a snow job? Who knows? . . . but it's interesting to get the other side.

"Along this line is the whole question of finding consultants and sticking with them until they've had a fair opportunity to demonstrate the quality of their work. The little people are often particularly weak here. Larger firms tend to be more sophisticated."

"Hold it right there." I wasn't at all sure I liked his condescending attitude, and I felt myself bridling. We're supposed to be the backbone of free enterprise; we make up the majority of employers in this country and have to be damn smart to make it. "When we call the best-known consulting outfits like yours for example, my experience is that you send us the second team. Frequently we get some 'wet behind the ears' junior, and frankly, I'm not sure how much supervision he or she gets from the heavies at the downtown office. Oh, sure, they read the reports, but they don't really spend any time on site. Then if we do get a good young man or woman who pleases us with the job, when we try to get that one back again he or she's either been promoted to bigger stuff or been transferred, and then we start with another novice. That's why I went the professor route. At least I get the same person each time, and I don't have to start with a 'brief history of our company.' "

"Now you wait a minute," shot back MacCormick, who was also getting aroused. "Sure we keep our good young people moving—that's the only way we can retain them. They get offers, not only from competitors, but even more often from clients. We *have* to give them assignments that both justify their salaries and keep them charged up. At our place, the files on each client are complete, so a new person reviews them thoroughly and is checked out before visiting the client; besides, all our people and all the reports we submit are thoroughly gone over by a senior person before they're sent out. That's the way all first-class management consulting firms operate; *we* are particularly strong here. The clients benefit from several levels of scrutiny and several professional opinions, not just one or two, as is the case with the part-timers."

"OK, OK, we're getting off the track," I put in somewhat self-righteously, because by this time I'd cooled down. "No question it's hard to choose a management consulting firm in the first place. You know the names of the biggies and you talk it over with friends who've used consultants, but in my view, it's like having your car repaired. You can go to a big dealership with its array of specialists, turn over your problems to them, trusting that a good one will work on your vehicle, or you can wait until a mechanic, a generalist I guess you'd say, who you're convinced is thoroughly competent can fit you into the schedule. It's a matter of choice, and it will always be debatable. Let's get back to giving consultants a fair chance to show their stuff."

"All right," replied MacCormick. "Consulting firms

and individual consultants get to know a lot about clients and their problems in the course of almost any assignment, and they build up a background of knowledge and information while performing their services. The more they know, the more efficient and the better they are. The consultant knows this and so should the client; yet periodically, with no discussion, explanation, or advance notice, consultants learn indirectly that another firm or individual has taken over. Fortunately this doesn't happen often to first-class outfits, but when it does, it's often because of misunderstanding which could be straightened out and result in considerable long-run savings to the client."

"Why do you think this happens?" I queried.

"In large companies, it may come about because there's been a shift at the top or the new high level executives had previously established a good relationship with the principals of another consulting firm. On the other hand, it may be because another division manager gave a rival firm a rave review, albeit on a simpler job; I'm not sure, but I suspect the same reasons apply in the case of smaller outfits as well, plus what you might call a greater vulnerability to a smooth selling job by a new outfit in town. Unless the consulting firm really is doing an inadequate job and this has been decided after an open frank discussion, changing horses in midstream is not only unwise, but expensive."

I didn't much like his comment about the vulnerability of small company CEOs to slick selling jobs, but then I'm sure his recent experiences have probably been with good-sized organizations. I decided to try to get to more neutral ground.

"Any difference in the kind of assignments you get from big companies?" I asked.

"Well, let me think," MacCormick reflected for a moment. "To some extent. Small companies are often more specific. By that I mean that the assignment may be almost entirely technical in nature: 'How can we deal with such and such a problem?' or 'We'd like to know what our people think about us. Would you design and conduct an attitude survey?' Larger companies can staff up for those jobs, though I'm not at all sure that it's always cost-efficient for them to do so. From large companies we often get broad assignments of the 'Take a look at our . . . operation' nature. 'Let us know what sorts of things we should be thinking about now that will put us in good position five years out, including the kind of organization we should have.' You know that kind of thing. We get the same assignments with small companies too, but not as often. Another difference is that in complex organizations, our reporting relationships are not always as clear as we'd like them to be. We're often uncertain as to exactly who the client is here: an individual or the company as a whole, and if it's the latter, to whom do we report, not just to submit the recommendations, but to whom are we actually responsible? To the board of directors? The president? What if we've never met them, but our recommendations involve them and don't reflect too well on our contact person? Suppose the problem we've been asked to deal with is really only a symptom of a much more basic one that merits attention at the top, and yet our contact person refuses for self-interested reasons to pass it on up? Oh, we've developed approaches to all these situations; we insist as much as we can on reporting to the top person, and we're generally successful, but it's hard sometimes to know just who that individual is in a complex organization and how to get to him or her so that the needed actions are taken. Contact is generally much easier in a small company because fewer levels and layers are involved, but even there we've run into difficulties and have discovered later in a project that our reporting relationships were not as clear as we thought they were at the outset."

"Interesting," I mused. "Other complaints?"

"Sure, I could probably go on for quite a while. In fairness though, we've learned to deal directly with the majority of them and to avoid most of the rest. The clients we've had for a long time are really easy. We have an open relationship and minimal difficulties."

"You don't feel they're all open with you?" I enjoyed prodding him gently. "When aren't they open? Give me an example."

"Hard to pick one out of the blue. Let me think a minute. Mind if I smoke?" I shook my head, and Mac-Cormick proceeded to stoke up his pipe with Amphora. He got it lit, puffed a few times, and began. "All right, suppose we have the top people gathered around for a corporate strategy review and formulation session. It may have been because we were initially called in to do just that, or it may be because we were called in to look at the organization structure and told them we had to back up and look at strategy before we could do much about structure. You know Chandler says strategy should come before structure.[1] No matter. Anyway, we start looking at what the present strategy—the basis used for making long-term decisions—is unclear to the decision makers." I sensed he was drifting a bit.

"How do you mean unclear?" I asked.

"Either it hasn't been written down, or if it has, it hasn't been kept up to date. If it's current, it hasn't been communicated to all who are called upon to use it. How's that for a glib answer? And even that doesn't go far enough. Corporate policy still has to be accepted as the decision criteria by the decision makers, and that's not always automatic either.

"Let's skip over those problems, even though they're crucial, God knows, and get back to openness," he went on. "Let's assume we're at the point where all of the executive committee members, the chiefs, whatever you want to call them, agree on what the present strategy actually is; as I've indirectly hinted, that's often quite an assumption in itself. Then we start looking at changes in external factors operating on the organization in terms of threats and opportunities—in that order because threats are so often the source of opportunities. . . ." There goes the professor in him again, I thought to myself, but this time he got back on the track by himself.

"Particularly if the CEO is running the session, there's a tendency to play down the threats, if they're likely to depress earnings a year or so out, or not mention some of them, either because the boss has previously suggested they're not significant or because the lords are afraid the king will shoot the bearer of bad tidings. Anyway, external threats *must* be discussed openly, but for hierarchical reasons these are often suppressed, and this particularly is true with an outsider present. That's what I mean. Or, at the strength and weakness discussion stage, there's a tendency to overstate the number and extent of organizational strengths and do just the opposite when it comes to weaknesses. Same thing, only this time the individuals involved in these internal aspects of an organization's operation are, or are seen as, responsible for them, and this creates another lack of openness."

"So what happens then, and what can a consultant like you do about it?" I asked.

"Well, unless someone moves in skillfully and sensitively, a less-than-optimal new strategy is formulated. As to what you can do about it, consultants who can gently probe and sensitively lead and channel discussions can do great work here. Sometimes we send two of our people on assignments of this kind: one to watch the content and the other to watch the process and try to make sure all the participants are as open as possible, to act as facilitator, to use the jargon. It's hard to do both jobs at the same time. We've got to have the whole story, as accurate and as unvarnished as possible, to do our work properly—just like physicians—and it wastes a lot of time and client money if people are not open and honest with us, as well as with each other. This tendency to make information available to us based on *their own inaccurate* perceptions of our need to know, now that's a complaint we have, or rather *I* have about quite a number of businesspeople. Want a nightcap?" he asked.

"Sure, I'll have a bourbon." MacCormick summoned a cabin steward and ordered a Johnny Walker Black for himself and a Wild Turkey for me.

He was on fire, that one. "Let me tell you another beef I've got, and I think this'll stir you up some," MacCormick went on. "It's when we do a careful, thorough, and objective analysis, a lot better than the clients could have done themselves, submit a superb report along with carefully worded operational recommendations, and the client compliments us on how it exceeds their most optimistic expectations, then decides to pick and choose which suggestions they are going to follow. This, when the whole thing has been set up to work as a totality and is highly interdependent, this gets my goat." MacCormick was getting worked up, and it was showing every so slightly, but he still presented a cool exterior, very cool indeed. Maybe that's a real asset in gaining and keeping clients' confidence, helps build an image as a capable and effective confidante, I thought to myself.

"I can understand your irritation when that happens, but you know what I think?" I guess we were probably both a bit quick on the trigger. Funny how much alcohol you can absorb on a long flight, what with a champagne dinner. I went on in my most soothing manner, "I think you feel a bit put down when an executive whom you consider less sophisticated than you are rejects some aspects of your brain child. I don't mind admitting I've done it myself, and I'll continue to do it periodically, I might add. Let me remind you of those important factors which *I* think you people often forget. And this applies to both low-overhead consultants, to use MacIntosh's name for professor-consultants, and the high-overhead outfits like yours. One, we're paying the bill and have every right to take all, some, or none of the suggestions; two, we know more about our business, its environment, and its peculiarities than you do; and three, when it's all over, you people can close *our* door and walk away. I know you help with the implementation of your recommendations, but your involvement with our firm is not as intense or as long-lasting as ours. We're held accountable for what we do, and we can lose our livelihood if your suggestions don't work out. You're able to move on to another client, just like a surgeon moves on to another patient . . . win some, lose some." That should shatter his composure, I mused. It got to him all right, but he handled it beautifully even though his color changed slightly.

"Let's both calm down a bit," he said with an almost paternal inflection. "Let me assure you we *never* forget you're paying the tab and have the *right* to do anything you want with our report. That's not the point. Any consultant, whether of the 'low-overhead' or of the 'higher' (by the way, that's more accurate than high-) overhead group, is genuinely concerned with the success of the recommendations. But it's not a matter of your 'right'; it's one of our sincere concern for the client's welfare. Sure, you know more about some aspects of your business than we do, particularly when it comes to individual organization members—frankness and a longstanding relationship help here, but we do view your operations in a more clinical way and can see interrelationships in a way you can't or won't. As to your accountability for our recommendations and our ability to walk away, I'm sure you could find some consultants somewhere who do this, but not an outfit like ours. We depend on our reputation for producing results to stay in business; that's the only really effective way of acquiring and maintaining sophisticated clients. We're both accountable, but each in a different way.

"One last comment on your conversation with MacIntosh. We're both getting tired and argumentative and ought to turn in. Consultants don't like being security blankets; that's OK for psychiatrists, but not for us." MacCormick stood up, stretched and added, "Sounding boards maybe, but not blankets. Good night, I enjoyed our chat." He shook hands and walked towards the stairs. Interesting guy, I thought to myself, smiling at him as he descended the stairway. His hair is too long for my tastes, bit of a smartass too, but sharp, damn it!

MACGUFFY

TAIL WINDS did compensate for our late start
from JFK, and our flight landed on time at
Heathrow. I hadn't expected to sleep much on the
trans-Atlantic flight, but this one was unusual. After a
nightcap in the lounge, I went back to my seat and
zonked out. Maybe all that talk with MacCormick and
MacIntosh was what did it!

We disembarked and I walked toward the terminal
only to find there was a half-hour delay before we could
clear Customs: probably the aftermath of all those years
with a Labour government, I thought. Anyway, I found
a comfortable seat, one of the benefits of getting off
early from first class, and I had a book. If I looked suffi-
ciently absorbed, that might discourage MacCormick
and MacIntosh from starting in on me again.

Just as I got into my murder mystery, I could hear the
waiting room start to fill up with the rest of the passengers and glanced up to see an attractive woman, evidently traveling alone, scanning the area for a place to
sit. She spied the empty space next to me and settled in
to wait for the announcement that we could proceed
through Customs. Out of the corner of my eye I could

see she was more than attractive; in fact, she was extremely good looking in an "outdoorsy" way. She was wearing a well-tailored gray suit. MacIntosh no doubt would have recognized the fabric, but to me it looked like the Jaeger outfit my wife picked up in British Columbia when we took the trip through the Rockies last summer. I turned toward her and introduced myself, noticing the unusual jeweled brooch she wore on her lapel.

"I'm Allison MacGuffy," she said, "on the first leg of a European trip like you, no doubt." I commented on her brooch, which was eye-catching.

"Been in the Sutherland family for years," she replied. "I was a Sutherland before I was married, and it's old; was originally used as part of the Highland dress, in fact. My father gave it to me when I was married."

"Is your husband joining you on this trip?" I asked and then wondered whether my interest might be misconstrued. God knows it's hard for someone who was raised by strict Lutheran parents to talk easily to a female traveling alone, but damn it all, she's a human being. Why can't I get over this . . . this nervousness I guess is what you'd call it?

"No, I'm a widow. Director of college recruitment and college relations for International Carbon. My husband, Rod, died ten years ago; we had two children, and I got to start my career a bit earlier than I planned," she added lightly. "I'm on my way to Britain and France to set up a college recruitment program which we need to staff our planned European expansions."

"How did you get into college recruitment?" I asked. Not much of a question, bet it sounded stiff, but then I'm a bit stiff, starchy too, like my parents, I suppose.

"Good question," she replied. She certainly is easy, poised, and an able conversationalist, but I haven't met many women executives, I thought. "I have to begin at the beginning. My dad was a business school professor until he retired last year. When I was looking at colleges, he urged me to study behavioral sciences at Mount Holyoke. He felt it was a good major, and I could specialize later, in grad school. Well, an eastern college was a pretty exciting place for a young woman from upstate New York, but I never made it to grad school; I got married instead. Anyway, ICC did send me to the Harvard summer program last year. After Mount Holyoke, I went with my husband first to Syracuse and then to New York City. When he died, I had to put bread on the table for the little MacGuffies. One of Rod's friends works for ICC, and he told me that because of their affirmative action program I might have a good chance with them. I applied, and after a few piddling jobs in personnel I got my present assignment. I've never been quite sure whether I would have moved up as quickly if I hadn't been a woman. Maybe I'd have gone up even faster! In any event, I'm pretty sure my sex was not disregarded," she added with a twinkle in her eye. "I have a good job, but I've earned my spurs. I'm well paid, not as well as I think I should be, and I still don't get to travel first class on long flights, like some of our corporate hot shots, and you too for that matter. But who knows? If the government leans on ICC hard enough, the top brass may feel it would be good to have a woman as vice president of human resources and if I got the nod then I might ride the corporate jet," she added half-jokingly. "But I'd have to feel I earned any job before I took it—no tokenism for me. I don't need money or perks that badly."

"If you don't mind my asking, does being a woman make your job harder?" I never miss an opportunity to get firsthand information.

"I really don't know," she quipped. "I've never been anything else. I suppose at first some people were a bit surprised to see a woman in my position, but a lot of my contacts are with university people. Perhaps because some of them have been hit so hard by lawsuits accusing them of sex discrimination, they really weren't taken aback too much. In all honesty I think quite a few people inside ICC were glad to see the government start to pressure its contractors to move women into positions of greater responsibility in the organization and welcomed my appointment. As for the others, I think most of them aren't unhappy with the way I've set up our operation with its systematic program of college visits using our staff and occasionally line representatives. We're good at college recruiting, and I can say this because I haven't been on the circuit myself on a regular basis for a couple of years."

"Sounds to me as though you've got it made, a pretty neat job, I'd say: occasional travel, a well-functioning staff that's gained the respect of its clients, good salary, and prospects." I wish life were that simple for me: scrambling for customers, browbeating suppliers, bucking unionization, meeting shipping schedules, fending off the government, and trying to have a few bucks left over at the end of the year. The woman's got a soft touch. "What are your tough problems?" I asked.

"Several. I don't mind problems if I can see any way of getting at them and working out an approach, but I have a few at the moment where I'm caught in the middle, like every other manager. For example, there's this 'boom or bust' thing. To do our work properly we have to maintain good relations with the colleges; in a sense they are our vendors, and we want *more* than our share of their top-quality products, particularly when the market is tight and when all the other recruiters want the same thing. Frankly we work hard at cultivating good relations with placement people and professors. They know their 'merchandise' better than we do: they've had more time to appraise the graduates. We get to know the university people and can tell whom we can trust as opposed to those who see the job only in terms of getting a placement at any cost, without regard for the individual's likelihood of succeeding. These relationships have to be carefully established and then maintained; to do this we have to be good steady customers who come back year after year with offers of employment."

"The students who are hired would have to feed back good reports about their jobs to their schools, too, wouldn't they?" I asked.

"Certainly, but apparently most of them do in our case. Then too, we don't have much to do with their subsequent careers after they are hired. Maybe we will some time, but we're really just getting into career planning at ICC. I hope to play a role there also. But back to the problem: when things get slack, one of the first things to get slashed is college recruiting. As I said, it's a boom or bust business, yet we have to keep making college visits if we're going to keep our good contacts in first-rate shape. During those low periods we really can get superb people. We have a lot less competition and we comb the corporation, call divisional people even if we haven't got requisitions, and try to sell them on these top-notchers. There are nearly always better qualified people in larger numbers than we could hope to get at any other time."

"Wait a minute. Wait just a minute," I interjected. "Divisional people are under tremendous pressure to cut costs when things turn down. Some of them are even thinking about laying off personnel, and you want them to keep hiring willy-nilly." She was going too far, that one. Don't personnel people ever have any knowledge of costs? "What would you have the division do?"

"I'm glad you asked. They should try to smooth their hiring out a bit," she replied. "We need the best people any time they present themselves with their hats in their hands, and we should hire them for the future regardless of the business cycle. On the other hand, I'm convinced we don't need a lot of the second-stringers we hire just to fill recruitment quotas when the market is tight. We could use overtime in some cases, I suppose, but more realistically, we should use interdivisional transfers to smooth things out. This we could do if we had a first-class managerial inventory that is kept really current. We started one a while ago, but divisional people lost confidence in it and started hiring outside rather than looking inside for the best qualified people. With a computer-based, up-to-the-minute inventory of corporate managerial talent, we'd make better use of our personnel and at the same time convince our people that superior performance is recognized on a corporate-wide basis. Oh, I know some managers would resist these transfers of their subordinates." She paused and then went on, "However, internal recruiting often produces better candidates than hiring from outside. Still, I bet our most profitable division would still continue to use the services of an outside employment agency. But just think how much more profitable they would be if they let us do it for them?" she added, only half in jest.

"What kinds of talent do you recruit and where do you find them?" I asked. Fred Jr. is going to grad school in a couple of years, and ICC is not an atypical recruiter. I might as well find out all I can.

"Sales people, some liberal arts, and some BBAs. I'm not sure a college degree really is a bona fide work qualification. Engineering degrees are, to be sure, but I have the lingering suspicion that a lot of the ones we hire are given initial assignments on the drawing board that should really be done by technicians and then promptly forgotten. The good ones leave as soon as they find that out, by the way. Engineers are touchy about their professional status, and I don't blame them! I think we often hire a higher level of talent than we need and get shocked when we have high turnover. And then there are the MBAs, 'the golden boys and girls of management.' We don't hire as many as we used to, but that's a story in itself, a pet topic by the way."

"Why is that a pet topic of yours? My son has been muttering about graduate business school recently, and I'm interested."

"Two-part question, two-part answer," replied Mac-Guffy. "It's a pet topic because we still hire them, and as I told you, my father was a business school professor although he was trained as an economist initially. As if that weren't enough I'm on the advisory board of the Business School at Mohawk State University, and I teach one evening course there. Although I think that board is the Dean's sop to the business community, which I suspect he views as a source of funds and placement, I have taken my appointment seriously and will continue to do so. Are you sure you really want to hear my opinion on this?"

"Uh huh. I do." Still no sign of activity at Her Majesty's Customs. I'm a damn good listener, although this trip has sure strained my abilities in that department!

"Well, let's begin at the beginning. A few years ago there was a kind of mystique about the degree, and this was naturally enough transferred to its recipients. . . ."

"I think I know what you mean," I interrupted. "There was a time I felt that it would have made my own job searches easier. Perhaps too, we've become even more credential conscious in this country over the past few years. I suppose when it comes to promotion, as well, the MBA has the inside track, not just because of knowledge, but also, if it doesn't work out, the choice can be more readily defended by the individual who made the recommendation. What do you think?"

"Uh huh," agreed MacGuffy, "and if they've gone to a half-decent business school, they've been exposed to a common body of knowledge. For example, marketing majors also know how to read a set of books, know the difference between debt and equity, and so on. But then, so does a BBA."

"Why the mystique then?" I asked.

"I'm not sure I can give you a precise answer. It's probably a mixture of things heavily related to a desire to professionalize management, maybe to give it more social standing and make it more comparable to law. Besides, the degree can be laid on engineers, to get them out of the technical stream and more directly into the management lines of succession. Except in a few organizations where the loss of high-quality engineering people into less-productive managerial assignments has forced them to rework their compensation and status systems, engineers typically make more rapid progress to the top end of the pay scale on the near managerial side.

"The graduating MBA is also more mature than the BBA, if only by virtue of age—much more so, of course; if there were a few years of real-world experience between undergraduate and graduate school. Incidentally, that's a real plus as far as we're concerned. For a time, at least, the possession of an MBA was seen by many, if not as a visa to upper management levels, at least as a passport which helped to reduce the waiting period for serious consideration. Many organizations got into the scramble for the annual crop of MBAs, bid up the price (incidentally causing difficult internal distortions in salary schedules), hired more than they needed, put them on jobs the new hires thought were below them, consequently suffered high turnover, hired even more the next year at even bigger salaries, disillusioning the crop harvested the year before and causing more turnover, and on and on it went.

"Eventually, and legitimately in most cases, I'd say, a goodly percentage of the higher management consisted of MBAs. A quick review of these people revealed one unique qualification they held in common. Even though heavily influenced by the organization's past hiring practices and their own MBA-based promotional recommendations, executives pointed to the high percentage of the top-level jobs in the company held by MBAs, and they continued hiring them to ensure, as they put it, an 'adequate supply of top-flight upper managers for the future.'

"This nonsense has cooled down considerably in the last couple of years at ICC at least, perhaps because of the salary differential as much as anything else, but I like to think it was because we're smartening up and becoming too sophisticated to be awed by credentials alone."

"What about the current crop of graduates?" I asked. "How do they stack up?"

"Those we've hired are technically proficient. They can all play 'Stars and Stripes Forever' on a computer terminal. They even know what 'boundary spanning' is, although practically no one else at our place does. And they're smart; competition for admission has increased, and those that get admitted are good test takers and exam writers at least. But I think they're becoming less practical and realistic about the real world of business. *You* know business is not as pure a science as physics; its practitioners must be application experts. It's not enough to know the paradigms that are currently in vogue; these change with surprising rapidity. MBAs should be sensitive to the world in which they are going to have to function, a very imperfect world when compared to the behavioral or the computer lab where everyone respects and even admires everyone else's expertise. I warned you this was a pet topic. You're sure you want me to continue?"

I did want her to continue, as she was getting quite interesting. And there was still no real activity beyond the brief appearance and almost immediate disappearance at the end of the Customs Hall of what looked like a Royal Naval Officer. "Why is this?" I probed.

"I don't think I'd have tackled that question six months ago, but after an active year on the Business School advisory board, during the course of which I've spent time looking at the curriculum, but more importantly, talking to professors, my ideas are clearer. In fact, I have my notes here that I hope to assemble into a report to my boss. Maybe I'll send it on to the dean, although he'll probably get all defensive and ignore it." Reaching into her briefcase to pull out a file of typed notes, she continued.

"First let me say that I think the problem is going to get worse before it gets better. Its roots go deep, and consequently its solution, which is what really interests me, will require some radical rethinking at all levels, particularly at the administrative levels which, in the short run at least, are the strongest influences on the value systems under which the business school functions. Let me be more specific. The real source of the problem is of course the professors."

"I'm confused. I thought you just said administrators are the strongest influences on a school's value system?" I asked. It sounded like a contradiction.

"In the *short run*, but in the long run, professors have the potential to change the administration even of an entire university and have done so. Have you ever been to a faculty meeting? Well I have—several, in fact, in the last couple of months. I'm overwhelmed, not only by the cumbersome nature and subsequently the snail-like progress to any conclusions, but also by the tremendous amount of rhetoric, the equal amount of politicking, and the seeming inability of the professors to take any real action. I assume this is an important reason why so much influence over the school, and hence so much responsibility for it, has gone to the administrators, aided no doubt by the success some strong deans have had in garnering increasingly scarce resources at the university level and from the public at large. According to my father, many deans, very few of them with any real-world management experience, feel they're expert managers; they see their function as manipulating power groups in order to achieve results that will bring credit to their own administrations and are not really sincerely interested in the teaching mission of their schools. The professors *can* effect change and occasionally do, but how can you get a group to agree on where to go to lunch if they can't decide whether or not they're hungry?"

"Let's get back to the value structure of a business school and its influence on the education of MBAs, which is our original concern," I reminded her. She gets carried away too, just like MacCormick—too much exposure to the academy, I guess.

"I was about to," MacGuffy countered. "It's not a simple question, and the answer as I see it is multifaceted.

Let's look at the professors' two principal areas of responsibility: teaching, and research and publication.

"Here, just a second while I glance over these notes. The most obvious point to be made in the teaching area," she continued, "is that, as with deans, surprisingly few business school professors have ever held a position of management responsibility in a nonacademic setting, and so they don't know much about the actual application or, perhaps more significantly, the nonapplication of the theories they teach in the real world. You know, in spite of having a father who was at a business school when I started at ICC, I was genuinely surprised by some aspects of the world of the manager, and so, incidentally, was my father when I discussed them with him."

"Like what, for example?" I asked.

"Any number of things, from the significant, like the importance of hitching your wagon to the right managerial star, executive politics, and hedging responsibility for mistakes as keys to promotion, to the trivial, like taking what is in reality an expensive and unnecessary business trip just to get away from the office for a while. In classes I've attended at State, I notice many of the teachers are hard pressed for examples to make their material real and interesting and have only their university experience to cite. I think that's one real reason why they focus their teaching on the latest fads or fashions, preferably the ones they're currently researching for eventual publication. Business is applications-oriented by its very nature, and so many professors, with the possible exception of the accountants, most of whom understand the operational uses of their own specialty at least, are blissfully ignorant of the practical applications of what they teach.

"Would you want to cross a bridge designed totally

by an engineer who had never been on a bridge construction site?" she concluded with a rhetorical question.

"What about those who do consulting? They're exposed to what you call the real world, aren't they?" I asked.

"It depends. Some are, some aren't. The real consultants, those who actually advise and take responsibility for their recommendations, gain insights. But there are also professors who call themselves consultants and whose outside work consists of continually repeating the same old 'dog-and-pony show' to different groups of executives and calling it management development. In most cases, this really doesn't help their teaching too much. Still, even real consulting isn't the same as holding down a full-time job and taking the whole responsibility, and periodically the blame, for your actions, but its' better than no experience at all. Another problem is that consultants, both the real ones and the dog-and-pony crew, often make a lot of money on the outside, and their teaching and counseling of students suffer from neglect."

"How about retired business people as business school professors or executives-in-residence?" I asked.

"They can really help here, but there are problems as well, and they're not the ones you might expect. Although they're not usually trained as teachers, they've done surprisingly well; at least that's what I gather from the people at State. The problems are in other areas; for example: professors with regular academic credentials often claim outsiders are not fully qualified to hold a regular appointment. Some universities, State isn't one of them, have stopped this nonsense, but in many business schools the insiders add insult to injury by putting down this teaching as anecdotal. No doubt they're weaker on theory, but they're strong on application. Then too, the real-worlders are often more willing to act as Big Daddy to students because the students are a novelty to them, and lecturers have a lot more time to do so than the regulars since they're not under the same publication pressure. Frankly, I think they're a real plus and are sorely needed. Their teaching is kind of a hobby. The same is true of the executives-in-residence, but I think this lot is often a bit more pontifical, at least from the ones I've heard at State. I suspect they embroider their accounts of their great managerial decisions. Anyway, they're both a breath of fresh air, but because of budget pressures and cutbacks they may suffer.

"But I think what really depresses me most about business schools is the low esteem in which teaching is held. What really counts is publication and research, in that order, incidentally. And I'm not just talking about State; I've spent a fair amount of time talking to professors across the country, and it's the same story most anywhere."

"Publish or perish?" I put in.

"I wish it were that simple, but it goes beyond that. Publish or perish really only applies to getting tenure. A young assistant professor has to show he or she is capable of doing work acceptable to peers outside of the university. If they're published in a 'respectable journal,' it means that their work was compared to the work of others seeking publication and judged by what are supposedly the top people in the field as being some of the best work submitted. Believe me, the rejection rate is frightening. It's an outside test of competence in and understanding of the field, and they have seven years to show this kind of competence."

"I can't see anything really wrong with that," I interjected. "It's kind of an apprenticeship period. After all, tenure really amounts to a life contract, which is more security than a manager has."

"That's fair," she agreed. "Up to now, I guess few tenured people have gotten the axe. I'm told the only traditional reasons have been incompetence, which I think would be almost impossible to prove, and moral turpitude. In the 1980s I'm not at all sure anyone even knows what that is! But now there's a new one, economic necessity, where whole programs have been eliminated. I might argue that in real life a lot of managers have more economic security than they might admit, and that seven years is a long time for what is often a middle-aged person to wait to know whether he or she has a job, but let's not get into that can of worms now! Anyway, setting aside the tenure-granting bit, the publication business has become the basis for virtually all personnel actions: promotion, salary increases, or membership in the graduate faculty, the latest wrinkle at State."

"Well," I countered, "it still seems pretty reasonable to me to rely on an outside judgment of professional competence as well as monitoring how a university professor fulfills the responsibility to advance the understanding of the field. Besides, when something is published, the audience is a lot larger than the classroom." I paused here, then asked, "How can you measure the effectiveness of teaching? My kids tell me that student evaluations are popularity contests. But you can measure publications: at least they're concrete or even quantifiable. Isn't that so?"

"Yes and no," she replied. "Let me answer the second part of the question first. Yes, it's easier to measure publication because teaching is not readily measurable, and you need several inputs to gauge it. Student evaluations, with all their faults (and there are many), are one source. More importantly, other professors get to know who is and isn't a good teacher; my father certainly could see which students were well prepared and which weren't. But you're right, it's not as quantifiable as publication. And there's one negative aspect of student evaluations that the assistant dean mentioned at an advisory council meeting. He said he was sure some of the school's personnel committees were using statistically insignificant differences in evaluation scores as a major basis for allocation of salary adjustments—pretty discouraging!

"But back to publication: there are problems in several areas, besides the obvious one that a professor has a fixed amount of time and what is spent on publication is not available for anything else," she continued. "And in all fairness, you can overdo that one; *some* researchers, but by no means all, are among the best teachers. They're obviously current, and they're excited by their subject. Meanwhile, others who consider teaching a nuisance and spend a lot of time trying to get out of it, manage to wheedle reduced teaching loads so they can step up their publication rate and hence their salaries and advancements—that seems a bit unfair, at least in my books. Then there are nonpublishers who teach the same stuff year after year and fall behind in their own discipline. So you can't really generalize. My point here is that, for good economic reasons, many professors turn to publication as the real priority. For them teaching is drudgery and below them; the students know it and suffer accordingly. But there's more to it than that."

"How's that?" She's really getting wound up now, talking faster and more intense, taking jacket off—tender spot here, maybe her father didn't publish. Still no action at H. M. Customs. . . .

"For instance, what gets chosen for publication. I'm really talking about journals now. Remember we talked about fads? I talked to a young doctoral student of my father's who finished up when Dad retired. She came for dinner the other night, and she gave us the scoop on general advice from a much-published colleague to young professors seeking publication. In her view, it really boils down to developing expertise in the latest analytical technique available, carefully revising it regularly to incorporate every minute refinement reported in the most esoteric journal available, and then applying it to everything in sight."

"I never see any of that in the journals I read, or damn little of it," I commented. What the hell is she talking about?

"Exactly, and that's another gripe of mine," she replied. "Precious few people in the real world do see that sort of stuff. The editors of the journals they do read know it's of no interest to their readers because of its limited applicability. Oh, I'm sure the subscription lists of the exotic journals so revered by business professors include company librarians and the odd executive who has the hots for the academy and likes to leave a few copies on display on his or her credenza, but whether they're ever read is another question. Academics write in these things to impress each other. I'm sure this is true in the sciences to an extent, but *real* application is the test of business research. Without it you've got a big zero, and frankly I wonder how many of the articles really have any impact on anything. Ironically, the journals that businesspeople read and are influenced by in their decisions are usually held in relatively low esteem by the effetes at the Business School of Mohawk State."

"Why do you think that is?" I questioned.

"I think that many professors, particularly those with

a completely academic background, feel that widely read business journals are too tainted with practicality. They've come to think that application is not as valuable as theory. Mind you, I'm certainly not arguing that theory is unimportant: clearly it provides the underpinnings for change and progress, but without real application and proof in the real world, it is an exercise and not much more. As I said, this theory emphasis forms the basis of so much of the teaching I've sat in on in graduate classes at State. You can see the effects in the unrealistic picture of the business world held by many of the young graduates, particularly those who have gone straight through with no work experience. Sir William Osler saw the danger of this in the medical schools of his time with their concentration on lab and lecture, and he radically changed medical education. In his valedictory address at Johns Hopkins, he said that teaching medical students in the wards was the most useful and important work he'd done.[1] Maybe there's a lesson here for business schools and their professors. Labs and classrooms and texts are useful, God knows, but somehow students have got to be better exposed to the real world. For example, sometimes students can work with the professor on actual cases involving current problems rather than historical cases; sometimes outside people can be brought in to talk to classes (incidentally businesspeople usually enjoy this and find it flattering); sometimes they can even go out with them on consulting assignments or do more work of this kind under supervision. The gap between the professor and the world has got to be closed. And when it is we'll all benefit: students and professors will be more realistic, and there will be greater opportunities for more valuable research. Business is applications-oriented; so should collegiate business education be, more like Osler's view of medical education, less like pure math. This should have more impact on the evaluation of research and publication as well."

"I gather you see a relationship between teaching and research; I wasn't sure you did," I commented.

"What I would call 'real teaching' and 'real research' in a business school are intimately related, but what's happened in many schools, if not most, is that research is directed almost exclusively at what is most likely to be accepted for publication in journals. It has little applicability to the real world and, when used as a basis for teaching, doesn't really help in the educational process. Perhaps its use is more justified at the PhD than the MBA level, but . . ."

"What sort of research can be integrated into MBA teaching?" I asked hurriedly, noticing a bit of activity at H.M. Customs, lines being set up, forms readied.

"Research done in the world of business. Case studies are the most obvious examples: analysis of actual problems executives are dealing with currently, design, discussion, administration of surveys. Not just learning of the existence and use of tools for analysis, but their applicability to and use in real situations and, most importantly, the interpretation of the data collected. Business history too provides insights—all this in addition to a thorough understanding of the functional areas. A tall order, isn't it?"

"All things considered, would you advise a college-bound person who wasn't interested in the traditional professions to give business school a try? Your child, for example?" Best question to get at the nub of my advice to Fred Jr.

"You bet. It's a good general education, but it would be better if we could only bring the academic and the business manager together. Maybe exchanges ought to be considered a lot more seriously, not just for summers or semesters, but a few hours a week in exchange for a seminar. I ought to look into that myself."

"One last question." I wanted to get this one in before we got to the Customs line. "If you had to choose between two young college grads, equal in all respects except that one was a man and one was a woman, and there was only one job available, who would you choose?" I'd always wanted to ask a woman executive that one.

"That old chestnut? Well, in real life there never are two candidates with equal qualifications, but if there were, I'd choose the woman," MacGuffy replied.

"Because of affirmative action?"

"That would be one good reason I suppose, but," she said with a smile, "the real reason is that she would probably work harder." Then she put on her jacket and gathered up her things.

"To prove herself?" I pursued.

"Maybe. More likely, though, she wouldn't be as distracted by our beautiful typists. We haven't been able to integrate our secretarial personnel yet; they're too sexist." Moving toward Customs, she gave me a parting smile and said, "Good luck!"

MacDuff

I'D FINALLY ended up buying an N.C. lathe at the
machine tool fair in Frankfurt. It was expensive
but worth it when I compared price, specifications, delivery date, and so on with anything else I saw. Those
damn Germans had been able to convince even a
hardnosed middle westerner like me that they'd provide at least as good and probably better service than
their U.S. competitor whose entire factory was a few
blocks away from their Cleveland distributor's ware-
house. I hate to admit it, but "Buy American" only goes
so far. Well, at least the numerical controls had a good
solid American name on them!

I'd always wanted to play St. Andrews, where the
whole golf business began, and I'd arranged to fly back
to the States from Prestwick on Monday so I'd have the
chance to play on a Sunday morning. It's not that I'm
very good; I guess I wanted to brag about it to a few
buddies at the country club in Toledo, but the prospects
of finding anyone to play with seemed pretty dim. I'd
had no trouble, even at 8:30 A.M., getting permission to
play and renting clubs, so I decided I'd wait for about
twenty minutes before I started out by myself. The

weather was cold and misty, but I wasn't going to miss this chance, that was for sure. Sitting myself near the starting tee, I took the opportunity to think back over the last leg of my European trip.

My reverie was cut short when, out of the corner of my eye, I saw rather than heard an immaculate vintage Rolls Royce limousine glide to a stop not far from where I was sitting. I was expecting to see a chauffeur slip out of the driver's seat and scurry over to open the rear door, but instead an older, very spry figure wearing gray flannels and a tweed jacket jumped out vigorously from behind the wheel, spied me, and walked briskly over.

"Looking for a game, young laddie?" he asked with just a touch of Scottish brogue.

It was a long time since anyone called me that, and I looked him over to try and size him up. He seemed to be in his mid to late sixties, thin, with a tanned lined face and sparkling blue eyes that missed very little, if anything, of what passed before them—wiry little guy, could be a good golfer, I thought to myself. "That'd be great," I replied.

"I'll be out of these duds in two shakes and we'll start out—no waiting line today." He strode off to the clubhouse, leaving me with my thoughts. I bet there's a story behind that Rolls; I suppose it's his, but how come no chauffeur? I wonder if he's retired? He looks prosperous enough—must be, to buy gas for that monster. How come he hasn't got a partner? Maybe he's a bore. I've heard there's no bore like an English bore, but then, he's a Scot, so maybe that's different. . . .

He reappeared more quickly than I'd expected, with plus fours, argyle socks, and sweater, and carrying a leather golf bag, obviously old, but in immaculate condition. He held out his hand.

"Duncan MacDuff's the name," he said. "What's yours, young chap?" I told him, and we shook hands vigorously.

"I usually play with the vicar," he explained, "but he has Sunday services, and it's hard to get anyone up at this hour. Best time of the day. Just came from eight o'clock church myself, hence the jacket and pants when I arrived." Then he saw me glancing at the Rolls out of the corner of my eye. "The car too, for that matter. I only take it out once a week or so—awfully hard on petrol, but I can't bring myself to sell it; it's been in the family so long. My father bought it over forty years ago," he said, glancing at it fondly. "It's a relic, like I am, I guess, and our lives have been intertwined. Well, let's get on with it." We walked on to the first tee, and we were off to a good start.

He was good, and a lot stronger than he looked, obviously no weekend golfer! It turned out he played four to five times a week, mostly with the "vicar," the local Church of Scotland rector, now semiretired and for many years a professor of philosophy at the University of Edinburgh. After six holes, of which I managed to win only two, he had found out all about me, my family, and my business—a good listener that one. I decided to turn the tables and find out all I could about him, which turned out to be interesting. MacDuff gave a brusque, but complete picture of himself and his career as I had done about mine, but he was better organized in his presentation and mildly self-deprecating about his accomplishments.

It turned out that he was older than he looked, seventy-five to be exact. He was from one of the outer islands off the coast of Scotland, the only child of a successful distiller who ran what later became a moderate-size operation producing single malt whiskey, some of which was sold directly and the rest to other large distilleries for blending purposes. MacDuff never went to university because his father took him into the business as soon as he finished secondary school. Apparently the elder MacDuff, an avid reader himself, felt a bit guilty about this, purchased the Harvard Six-Foot Shelf of Books, and made it his mission to read them himself, one by one, before handing them to his son for reading and subsequent discussion. "My father was of the old school. He was a bit frightening, and you can be sure I was prepared for those discussions," said MacDuff with some admiration. "I learned a lot from him, not only from the reading we did together, but also about the business and how it could be made successful. Maybe he formed me in his own image," he added with a wry smile.

Evidently the MacDuff enterprise prospered. I confess I'd never heard of his product's retail name, but then I'm a bourbon man myself. The young MacDuff spent a considerable amount of time in England and eventually a London sales office was opened, and the Rolls Royce appeared on the scene, with chauffeur. When World War II came along, he joined the Sutherland Highlanders (that was curious, with Allison MacGuffy née Sutherland and all), and the Rolls was put in storage. He served in the Army until early 1945, when he was discharged after extensive service in Europe. Both parents having been killed in an air raid while staying in London, MacDuff, Jr. became president of the family company, married after the war, and put the Rolls back on the road, still with a chauffeur paid by the company. He divided his time between the London office and the distillery.

The postwar increase in demand for all Scotch whiskey, which he said was more significant than his native

Scottish business acumen, resulted in a sharp increase in the size of the operation. In the early sixties he purchased a cottage near St. Andrew, where he now lived alone since his wife's death three years ago. In 1965, as he had no children, he reluctantly decided to sell his business to a large Canadian distiller who needed its entire production for blending purposes and was willing to guarantee continued employment to all the workers on the payroll, a provision he had insisted upon. In fact, because of the subsequent growth of the business, it proved to be of no real significance.

MacDuff was retained as a consultant until his retirement at age sixty-five, ten years previously. During this period he spent a considerable amount of time at the New York office. He said he continued to keep in touch with the "lads in the States," as well as with a few of his friends at the old distillery, and that he spent a lot of his time reading business periodicals, rereading the Harvard classics and talking to his cronies, particularly the vicar.

"But that's all history," concluded MacDuff, after the first nine holes. He'd beaten me soundly, and I considered myself lucky to have won three holes, but then he knows the course and plays more often than I can, I rationalized. "Now that we've gone over all that, and we understand a bit about each other," said MacDuff, "tell me about what interests a young fellow like you. I'm isolated up here with my books and a few friends, and I don't get to meet businessfolk very much anymore. What kinds of things do you lads and lassies talk about when you get together?"

Well, that started it, and I spilled out summaries of the conversations I'd had on this trip, starting with MacCallum, then the two with MacCormick, whom MacDuff knew by reputation, MacIntosh, and finally Allison MacGuffy. He listened intently, zeroing in on particular points with penetrating questions, but never commenting himself. I was surprised how well I recalled the dialogues.

I'd like to think I hit my stride in the second nine. Maybe I did, but more likely MacDuff's interest in my account distracted him. For the record, I won five of the last nine, and I guess it was unsportsmanlike, but I did feel better about myself. I'm kind of competitive by nature.

We were walking back from the eighteenth green when MacDuff stopped, faced me with those lively blue eyes of his, and said, "You ought to record those conversations some time. Come on, I'm going to buy you a real drink."

Instead of moving off in the direction of the clubhouse, he steered me over to the spot where he'd parked his car, unlocked the rear door, and asked me in. Sliding in next to me, MacDuff reached forward and opened the hardwood cabinet built into the back of the chauffeur's compartment. He extracted a cut glass decanter and two matching glasses. "I'll not allow anyone to add ice or water to this—it's the best. Drink up," he said. "There's more where this came from."

Well, as I said, I'm a bourbon man myself, but I'd never tasted anything like it before. It was sneaky all right, but oh, so smooth. "Where can I get stuff like that?" I asked innocently.

"You can't, but I'll give you a bottle before you go. The boys at the distillery still send me a supply for myself. It's not on the market any longer, but employees can still get it for their own use. I made sure of that when I sold out!"

We stretched out in the sumptuous back seat which looked like a corner of one of the small members' rooms at the Toledo City Club. "Tell me about this car. I can see it's a Rolls . . . ," I began.

"Love to. It's my pride and joy, as I'm sure you'd guessed by now, and it takes more of my time and effort than it should. No chauffeurs anymore, so I keep it up— the coach work that is—myself. It's a Rolls-Royce Phantom III; made for my father in 1936, has a V-12 $7\frac{1}{3}$-liter engine, and will do an honest 100 miles per hour. The chassis weighs just over two tons, and the body was made by Hooper. The gas tank holds thirty-three Imperial gallons, and it needs every one of them; that's its only fault as far as I'm concerned. In my view, it's the best car ever built—total integrity in design and execution. A bit old fashioned I suppose, but I'm old fashioned too for that matter. . . ."

"You don't drive this every day; you said it was mostly for church. What's your other car?" I interrupted.

"A Morgan Plus 4, a hard-riding two-seater, built by Peter Morgan's crew in Malvern Link. Externally the opposite of the Rolls in every way, internally the same— total integrity in design and execution. That's what really counts in my book, always was my goal and still is," MacDuff replied. He added a generous dollop to my glass, but still had barely touched his own. How easily that went down! I was so relaxed, and that car! Fred Jr. will want to hear all about it. MacDuff is good company too. Stretching out full length and sinking back into the cushions, I wondered what that little Scot next to me really thought of my outpourings on the golf course, but I didn't have long to wait for my answer.

"You know, when I heard you spinning that yarn about those lads and that lass that you talked to, I had a tremendous feeling of nostalgia for my old life. MacCallum was clearly a new school manager who'd given a lot of thought to the motivation of high quality subordinates. I guess at this stage I'd feel that he should have specified ethical constraints on their behavior. . . ."

"How do you mean?" I asked.

"Well, take the petroleum industry. I don't know much about it other than what I see off the coast in the North Sea and from what I read of their enormous profits, which seemed to increase for so many years, in your country at least, according to pretty reliable publications. The public seems to be willing to pay whatever they have to for their products and with a few exceptions tolerate the obscenity of the destruction of their coast and shoreline just so they can motor down to the greengrocers in their own autos rather than take a bus, or ride a bike like I've begun to do again after sixty years or so," he said with a somewhat self-righteous snort. "You know it's simple greed on the part of the oil magnates, and it seems to me that eventually an inflamed public, in the democracies at least, is going to demand even more government intervention in their business. The oil giants, of course, will cry out in expensive advertisements, paid for by the consumers whom they have exploited, that it's the government, not they, who are destroying free enterprise." He was getting worked up.

I was about to ask him whether he knew any other better system than the one that had served the free world and him (with his Rolls Royce), but before I could get my act together, he went on. "Getting back to Mac-Callum, it seems to me that in any kind of delegation, the superior must specifically establish, preferably in writing, the ethical standards required of the subordinate. Mind you, it was no problem in a small operation like ours. Everyone knew what the family stood for, and they knew us personally, but in a large impersonal operation, my guess is ethical standards aren't set at all. The workers are expected to produce. The how is less important, and it's no wonder payoffs, shoddy workmanship, pollution, high prices, and the rest of it are becoming a hue and cry of various vocal segments of society. I suspect that ethical standards are only discussed when there's a scandal of some kind like the Phases of the Moon conspiracy a few years ago."[1]

"What about MacCormick the consultant?" I probed. "Any further comments?"

"As I said earlier, I've heard of him, and I wish I could have met him myself. His detachment seemed almost clinical though, but I suppose that's part of what you pay a consultant for. From what you told me, I'd say he sounded a bit defensive. He too left out specification of ethics in MBO systems, but then maybe, at his level of analysis, their impact is seen primarily in his emphasis on the long run rather than the short run. As I said, in the long run, without some form of constraint—either internal, in the form of some *real* commitment to something other than mere profit for profit's sake, or external in the form of ever-increasing government regulation—the public will be disadvantaged and the system will fail. . . ."

"And MacIntosh, the young president?"

MacDuff was talking easily, yet precisely. "Young MacIntosh has the right idea with his emphasis on quality, my type of laddy. I'd be careful about overexpansion if I were he; somehow it's hard to keep emphasizing quality when you get too big. Maybe it's because your vision narrows and all you look at is what MacCormick calls short-term operating results as a way of toadying to the financial analyst. But in my view, people are still willing to pay for quality, and some firms do retain high quality in spite of substantial size, like

Yamaha in stereo equipment, or Mercedes-Benz—ironic isn't it that Daimler Benz is controlled by a bank? Maybe banks necessarily stress the long term. Firms with a quality emphasis do seem able to weather adverse economic conditions and remain profitable too. In spite of their new plant in your country, I'm told you still have to wait for some Mercedes products. I remember I had to do quite a bit of hunting around to get my Yamaha audio equipment, and it was more expensive than its competition. Then there's Michelin—well, I could go on but I won't bore you."

"How about Ms. MacGuffy and her ideas on MBAs?"

"Bright lass that, reflective too. I couldn't argue much with her because she was discussing an area I don't really know much about. I bet she's a corker though. You know I've never talked to a woman in an executive slot? I'd find it unsettling, but then, it's been a while since I've been in business, and I suppose I haven't been able to get used to it. Still, I hope today's young women don't feel bearing children is below them. Wish I'd been able to leave the business to a child of my own, but that wasn't to be. Anyway, I'm not doing badly, and I haven't much to complain about really."

"No, probably not. . . ." I took another sip of that wonderful Scotch. "MacGuffy did have two children," I reminded him. "Children don't prevent men from having executive careers—that's what she'd tell you." I guess I wanted to prolong our discussion for a few more minutes as much as I wanted to hear him answer a question that's been forming itself with increasing clarity in my mind over the last two years. "You've had time to think this over, so I'd like to have your views on the future of free enterprise." That ought to set him on his heels, I thought to myself.

"I wondered whether you'd come up with that one,"

MacDuff said with a wink. "And I have to confess I'd hoped you would. It's something I've thought about a lot recently and discussed at great length with the vicar. I think it can survive; he doubts it, but then he's a bit of a parlor pink. Maybe he fell into bad company at the high table at his college. Anyway we get into heated discussions each time we get on to the topic. You think free enterprise is in trouble?" he asked, neatly turning the tables. "Why?"

Now I know what they mean when they refer to Scots as wily. There he is at seventy-five sitting complacently in the back of this living room on wheels and expertly tipping the ball back into my court to catch me off guard. Yet, damn it all, he's been hinting pretty strongly that he thinks capitalism may be in danger. "Maybe because the Puritan ethic is dying," I blurted out clumsily.

"In what way?" he asked. I had the disturbing feeling he was playing me like a trout in a Highland brook to give him a bit more line, and I was beginning to feel snagged.

"People dont' want to work as hard as they did when I was younger," I explained. "We took any job rather than be idle. Today, at least in the U.S., they'd rather go on welfare than do work that they consider below them. Something's happening to the Puritan ethic," I repeated.

"I agree that something has indeed happened to it," he replied. Why do I feel so put down by this character? He's genial enough, and I find him attractive. At least I've wriggled out of that one, not for long though. "Every generation has said that, probably even before the time of the Greeks, when I first saw reference to the idleness of the young, and if it were true, there'd have been no such thing as human progress. No, I can't accept that part of it. There have always been and probably will be loafers in any generation. No, in my view, that's not the fly in the free enterprise ointment."

"But you said you did agree that the slow death of the Puritan ethic was a factor affecting the ability of free enterprise to survive." At least I'm off the defensive with this guy. He is sticky, no question about that.

"So I did, but there's a lot more to the Puritan ethic than hard work. I don't feel qualified to give a definitive lecture on the subject; the vicar's the man for that job! But what you American businesspeople often seem to slide over is the Puritan concept of the 'elect,' the people whom they believed God had singled out for special recognition, one aspect of which was economic reward. This economic reward, however, brought with it responsibility, including the duty to live more modestly than their financial condition would otherwise have permitted. But I think what's particularly important about the Puritan ethic is the notion of *responsibility* and the constraints the 'elect' felt upon their behavior, and to an extent (just how great an extent I'm not prepared to say) this curtailed their unbridled greed. It is just that unbridled greed which, in my view, threatens the survival of free enterprise, and on this point the vicar and I do agree."

"I don't think it's true that capitalists as a group are greedy," I said, trying to keep my face from reddening. This was too much: here was this little Scot sitting back and relishing the good life that had been made possible by free enterprise while he condemned its advocates and proponents as greedy. "Some may be greedy, but most of the ones I know are not. Maybe they are here and that may be why you're always flirting with socialism on this side of the Atlantic," I said, a little self-

righteously. I don't like breaking my rule of never in-
sulting my host, even in his car, but there is a limit!

"Hold your horses, lad. Let's not get into that kind of
discussion! Don't forget Lieutenant Chauvin was
French, not American, and don't go learning bad habits
from the French." I could hardly hold back a smile—
skillful conversationalist that little golfer. "Of course I
agree with you that not all capitalists are guilty of unbridled greed. What I *am* saying is that unbridled greed,
exacerbated by what my fellow countryman, MacCormick, fears is a preoccupation with short-term financial
results to woo the speculator and the investment fund
manager, may well lead to the destruction of the capitalist system as we know it. As has been said a million
times, freedom always, in all ways, involves responsibility. When the populace sees, or even senses, for that
matter, that political and economic leaders are acting
in a manner that is irresponsible in terms of its welfare,
changes are made, sometimes bloodlessly, sometimes
not. The process usually takes place more slowly and
less violently in a democracy, but it takes place just the
same. Up to now, at least in western countries, capitalism has shown itself to be reasonably adaptive and
adaptable, but it is my belief that our system may be
facing its greatest tests in the next decade."

"Can you be more specific?" I asked, enjoying the
chance to put MacDuff on the griddle for once.

"I'll try. You mentioned that MacCormick is concerned about the short-run emphasis of many operating
executives. Of course, this emphasis has an impact on
the consumer, since it can result in overpriced goods
that may be designed for profitable manufacturing
rather than customers' needs. That was one good thing
about the single malt industry, by the way: our customers knew what they wanted, and we had to give it to

them, but it goes deeper than that. Corporate irresponsibility shows itself in so many ways that it's hard to decide which ones to mention. Pollution stands out: the Love Canal business and the danger it posed cannot have been totally unknown to the executives involved or, if it was unknown, it certainly indicates incompetence to me! Then too, firms often deliberately ignore health hazards faced by their employees, and it's not just the mining companies. I read a fascinating book a few years ago on this topic, muckraking as you'd say in America, called *Muscle and Blood*[2] in which the dangers of beryllium, coal tars, lead, asbestos, and so on, to workers' health were ignored by management who, in my view, should have been more responsible. Another example of irresponsibility is the way long-service workers are often laid off indiscriminantly when factories are relocated because of special tax concessions and lower wage levels offered by different regions, or even countries nowadays, to entice business into their backyards. I refuse to buy the argument that economic considerations should be more significant determinants of corporate decisions than responsibility to workers, but then, I always viewed our people at the distillery as more than factors of production. They were partners, and we were mutually dependent."

"Sounds paternalistic," I chided.

"I prefer to think of it as responsible," he replied sternly. "It seems to me that there are at least two reasons for treating workers in this way. First and obviously, the humane characteristics. The vicar always stresses the brotherhood of man—fatherhood of God argument, and we've discussed this matter many times. But the other reason has nothing to do with religion; rather, it's the most effective way to shore up the economic system that, up to the present time, has served our countries extremely well, I might add. If capitalism, or rather capitalists, behave irresponsibly, or as I said are even believed to be behaving in this manner, I think the jig is up, and free enterprise will be so modified and changed that it will be unrecognizable to us who knew and thought we respected it."

"Any advice for American business?" I sensed that the appropriate moment for me to end this discussion was approaching; I'd finished my second drink, and one more would lay me out on the impeccably clean woolen carpet on the floor of that elegant car. "I wanted to see the inside of the clubhouse before I went back to the hotel. Would you join me for lunch?" I asked.

"No thanks, lad. I'm going fishing in an hour or so—otherwise I'd love to. As for advice to business from an old Scotch distiller, well, let's see—I'd just quote their own management seer, Drucker, back to them. In fact, I memorized this quote because I was so impressed by it: 'Profit is not the purpose of but a limiting factor on business enterprise and business activity. Profit is not the explanation, cause or rationale of business behavior and business decisions, but the test of their validity.'³ To this I'd add only that profit must be seen as one vital, but not the only, responsibility of management. Managers must also face up to responsibilities to the customer to deliver a product of quality and integrity at a just price, (you know, I still believe St. Thomas Aquinas on this, even though I'm blessed if I know how you could go about calculating it), to the stockholders who risked their money in the venture, to the employees who make operations possible, and to the state and society which give it birth and whose laws protect and constrain it. Sounds old-fashioned, but what do you expect? So am I."

Leaning over, he took my glass and his to put them

back in the locker with the decanter, then retrieved a full bottle of Scotch which he handed to me.

"I think you'll enjoy this, lad," he said. "Here's the bottle I promised you."

I looked at the plain white label which read "MacDuff Private Stock Single Malt, Pot Still, Scotch" and in small letters "Quality and Integrity." I thanked him as I stepped out of the car. After shaking hands and wishing me good luck, he slid into the driver's seat, and the Rolls purred down the driveway.

I ambled back to the clubhouse, and as I approached the door, a waiter smiled and said to me with a burr, "I seen ya talkin' wi' Mistur MacDoof—they ma' qui' a cupple, him and that carr o' hiss'n."

"No doubt about that," I replied. "Quality and Integrity," I thought to myself, not bad. Maybe that's what's made capitalism work up to now. Enough of that. God, I hope I'll have a single seat on the plane back tomorrow, because I sure could do with some time to myself. I'm listened out.

NOTES

PREFACE

1. Jerome Bruner, *On Knowing: Essays for the Left Hand* (New York: Atheneum, 1976, originally published by Harvard University Press, 1962).
2. Joseph Litterer, *Chancellor's Address Series* (Amherst, Mass.: University of Massachusetts, 1975).

MACCALLUM

1. Henry Mintzberg, "The Manager's Job: Folklore and Fact," *Harvard Business Review* (July–Aug. 1975), p. 49.
2. Stanley Young, *Management: A Systems Analysis* (Glenview, Ill.: Scott, Foresman and Company, 1966), chapter 3.
3. Alfred D. Chandler, *Strategy and Structure: Chapters in the History of the Industrial Enterprise* (Cambridge, Mass.: M.I.T. Press, 1962), chapter 4.
4. This is a common means of showing changes in managerial duties at increasingly higher levels in the hierarchy.

5. Vincent S. Flowers and Charles L. Hughes, "Why Employees Stay," *Harvard Business Review* (July–Aug. 1973), p. 49.
6. Jerome S. Bruner, *On Knowing: Essays for the Left Hand* (New York: Atheneum, 1976), introduction.
7. George S. Odiorne, *Management and the Activity Trap* (New York: Harper & Row, 1974), chapter 1.
8. Chandler.
9. Frederick Herzberg, "One More Time: How Do You Motivate Employees?" *Harvard Business Review* (Jan.–Feb. 1968), p. 57.
10. Edward E. Lawler III and J. Richard Hackman, "Corporate Profits and Employee Satisfaction: Must They Be in Conflict?" *California Management Review* (fall 1971).
11. D. S. Sherwin, "The Meaning of Control," in Max B. Richards and William A. Nielander, eds., *Readings in Management* (Cincinnatti, Oh.: South-Western Publishing Company), p. 392.
12. Phil N. Scheid, "Charter of Accountability for Executives," *Harvard Business Review* (July–Aug. 1965), p. 88.

MacCormick

1. Joseph Litterer, *Chancellor's Address Series* (Amherst, Mass.: University of Massachusetts, 1975).
2. Frederick W. Taylor, *Scientific Management* (New York: Harper & Row, 1947).
3. Cited by Alistair Mant, *The Rise and Fall of the British Manager* (London: Pan Books Limited, Macmillan Press Ltd., revised edition, 1979), p. 4.
4. Harvey Sherman, *It All Depends* (University, Ala.: University of Alabama Press, 1966).
5. George S. Odiorne, *MBO II* (Belmont, Calif.: Fearon, Pitman Publishers, 1979).
6. Elliott M. Estes, *World Wide Competition—Can the U.S. Meet the Challenge?* (Philadelphia: Wharton Entrepreneurial Center, 1979), p. 4.

7. Stanley Young, *Management: Alternative Realities*, forthcoming.

8. Peter F. Drucker, *Management: Tasks, Responsibilities, Practices* (New York: Harper & Row, 1973).

9. J. Patrick Wright, *On a Clear Day You Can See General Motors: John Z. De Lorean's Look Inside the Automotive Giant* (Grosse Point, Mich.: Wright Enterprises, 1979), p. 191 and *passim*.

10. John Kenneth Galbraith, *The New Industrial State* (Boston: Houghton Mifflin, 1978).

11. *International Herald Tribune*, April 23, 1980, p. 10.

12. Wright, p. 191.

13. Frank A. Weil, "Management's Drag on Productivity," *Business Week*, December 3, 1979, p. 14.

14. A profit level of 1 percent after taxes was reported by Kawasaki Steel for the year ended March 31, 1979, according to R. P. Simmons, President of Allegheny Ludlum Steel Corporation, Pittsburgh, in *Business Week*, February 26, 1979, p. 4.

15. Cited by William C. Norris, "Ideas and Trends," *Business Week*, January 23, 1980, p. 20.

16. Alfred D. Chandler, *The Visible Hand* (Cambridge, Mass.: Belknap Press, 1977).

17. William E. Bonnet, vice president of technology, Sun Oil, cited in *Business Week*, February 16, 1976, p. 56.

18. *Intercollegiate Case Clearing House*, 9-373-337, revised 6/74, p. 9.

19. Theodore Levitt, "Marketing Myopia," *Harvard Business Review* (July–Aug. 1960), p. 45.

20. Robert Ludlum, *The Matarese Circle* (New York: Bantam Books, 1980), p. 538.

21. *International Herald Tribune*, May 7, 1980, p. 15.

22. *The Boston Globe*, February 27, 1981, p. 23.

23. Peter Drucker, *The Practice of Management* (New York: Harper & Row, 1954), p. 353.

24. Ibid., p. 354.

MACINTOSH

1. T. S. Eliot, *The Cocktail Party*, in *The Complete Poems and Plays*, 1909–1950 (New York: Harcourt Brace and Company, 1952), p. 306, l. 8.
2. Peter F. Drucker, *The Practice of Management* (New York: Harper & Row, 1954).

MACCORMICK II

1. Alfred D. Chandler, Jr., *Strategy and Structure* (Cambridge, Mass.: M.I.T. Press, 1962).

MACGUFFY

1. "I desire no other epitaph—no hurry about it, I may say—than the statement that I taught medical students in the wards, as I regard this as the most important work I've been called on to do." *Journal of the American Medical Association*, 44 (1905), p. 709.

MACDUFF

1. "The Incredible Electrical Conspiracy," *Fortune*, April 1961, p. 132; May 1961, p. 161.
2. Rachel Scott, *Muscle and Blood* (New York: E. P. Dutton, 1974).
3. Peter F. Drucker, *Management: Tasks, Responsibilities, Practices* (New York: Harper & Row, 1973), p. 60.